CHURCH POLITICS

Pain-Free Decision-Making

ALSO BY KENT R. HUNTER

A Nation Reclaims Respect: One Person at a Time

The Amazing Power of God Stories: Share What God Has Done in Your Life

An Apple a Day: A Daily Dose for Everyday Faith

Who Broke My Church? 7 Proven Strategies for Renewal and Revival

Discover Your Windows: Lining Up With God's Vision

Your Spiritual Gifts: Discover God's Plan for Your Life

The J-Dog Journey: Where Is Life?

The Jesus Enterprise: Engaging Culture to Reach the Unchurched

Your Church Has Personality: Find Your Focus – Maximize Your Mission

CHURCH POLITICS

Pain-Free Decision-Making

"For it seemed good to the Holy Spirit and to us...."

Acts 15:28a

Kent R. Hunter

with Tracee J. Swank

How would you make decisions

if Jesus was your pastor?

Cover Design by PixelStudio, Fiverr.com/PixelStudio
Cover Copyright © Church Doctor Publishing
Formatted by Church Doctor Publishing

ISBN: 979-8-39-604815-7

Printed in the United States of America

PRAISE FOR
CHURCH POLITICS: PAIN-FREE DECISION-MAKING

"Finally! A book written to help church leaders and board members rethink their governing structures and decision-making ethos. Dr. Hunter has done it again and provided the church with a resource that will guide leaders toward a biblical, functional, and liberating model of church governance. If you are an overseer in the church or oversee a collection of churches, *Church Politics* will be an invaluable resource for you as you help the church build effective leadership systems."

Ed Love, director of church multiplication for the Wesleyan Church and author of *Fear Not*

"Church governance and its biblical roots are overlooked topics among church leaders, but not anymore. Dr. Hunter, in this easy-to-read book, combines an appreciation for tradition along with biblical foundations to create a clear strategy for effective decision-making."

Bob Whitesel, church consultant with 32 years of experience, award-winning author/scholar, and directional leader of www.Leadership.church

"A book that will move you out of your apathy and misunderstanding about how a church is governed. The rewards will be immeasurable. It is great, but may receive some negative feedback from the Pharisees. This book needs to be shared."

Franklin Grepke, author of *The Malady of American Christianity*

"Churches, mission agencies, and ecclesiastical structures increasingly struggle with governance issues. By adopting methods from the secular and business world, Christian leaders encounter political division, power struggles, scandals, character attacks, and infighting.

In *Church Politics*, author and church consultant Kent Hunter addresses the important issue of church governance from a biblical perspective. He emphasizes the importance of solving problems through a focus on authentic relationships made possible by the power of the Holy Spirit working through God's Holy Word and nurtured through a renewed focus on the liberating Gospel of Christ.

This helpful book demonstrates how Gospel-centered decision-making and a commitment to a relational approach can help Christian leaders move away from rule-based decision-making to one led by and empowered by the living God."

B. Steve Hughey, mission consultant

"As a church consultant I have read well over five hundred sets of local church bylaws since 1982. Some have been close to the New Testament order, but most are geared to issues of control when governing the local church. *Church Politics: Pain-Free Decision-Making* is a great effort to remain true to the Scriptures and help local church leaders follow biblical structure. Get copies of this book and have your governance team read it and follow the plan."

Dennis L. Kutzner, general overseer, CMI Global

"Decision-making according to God's will rather than human votes: a great help for any church!"

David Maier, past Michigan District president,
Lutheran Church—Missouri Synod, and
founding member of Mission Partners Platform

"When an 'organism' like the church chooses institutional survival over Christ's mission, one can hear the death toll ringing. The focus of a Christian institution should be to support and expand Christ's mission. Dr. Hunter focuses this truth by looking at how congregations do governance. He challenges us in our comfortableness with the Word of God and commends a model which may fly in the face of what many of us have done for years."

Kip Tyler, senior pastor,
Lutheran Church of the Master, Omaha, NE

Dedicated to those who
subordinated politics
to focus on movement

I thank God for your influence on me.
God knows who you are.

Jesus
Paul
Martin
John
Billy
Lyle
Jim
Bill
Robert
Rick
Uma
Leroy
Peter
John
Elmer
Dave
Mick
Anthony
Andy
Nicky
David
Jon
Jason
Mark
Brian

CONTENTS

The *natural* drift of every church is from organism to organization; from governing to ruling; from prayer to politics; from Scripture to constitutions; from divine guidance to human bureaucracy.

The *supernatural* renewal for every church is released through biblical decisions made by spiritual leaders committed to the King of the universe: Jesus, the Head of His church, which is His body.

INTRODUCTION

> For twenty-five years I've taught pastors that "the church is a body, not a business. It is an organism, not an organization! It is a family to be loved, not a machine to be engineered, and not a company to be managed." Pastoring is an art. It has nothing to do with being a CEO. It's all about servanthood and authenticity and taking risks in faith.
>
> — Rick Warren[1]

The Christian movement can mutate to organizational religion.

God works through people. Nowhere in Scripture does it say God works through an organization.

Ever feel the pain of politics at church or in your denomination? After working with more than 1,800 congregations in seventy-eight denominations and in nondenominational and independent churches, and after training pastors and church leaders on six continents, one thing is clear: There is often a propensity to create non-biblical decision-making structures that divide, discourage, and disrupt the effectiveness of the Christian movement.

One of the greatest tragedies of Christian history occurs when human beings recreate their church in their own image. From the early days of the Roman Catholic Church to the various streams of Christianity birthed in the Protestant Reformation, human beings consistently seem to make the church an *organization.*

Anyone who gets involved in church "politics" knows it doesn't work out well. Just ask any pastor or burned-out church leader. Most have suffered from stressful meetings for years. Of course, they are *committed* to God's work. However, the stress often makes them feel like they ought to *be committed*—to an institution. It's that bad!

The greatest tragedy? Non-biblical approaches to church governance don't simply stall the operation of the local congregation. They rob God's unique entity, the church, of its power to be effective. God launched a *movement*, the divine dynamic to effectively reach the world for Jesus Christ.

When the spiritual *movement* of Christianity becomes an *organization*, it loses much of the supernatural power—the Master's transformational plan for impacting the world, one person at a time. Consequently, churches stall. Whole denominations wane. *Christianity actually declines because it is over-organized.* The faith loses its movement ethos. Why? We say Jesus is in charge. Yet, what do we do? We develop mechanisms of *control.* Boards, committees, councils, and consistories become the head of the church—even when Jesus is "invited" through the opening prayer. In the book *The Council: A Biblical Perspective on Board Governance*, the authors are clear: "When a group tries to control and rule over work that belongs to God, it is just a matter of time before things will unravel!"[2]

There is a tendency for human beings to pollute their sacred churches with organizational, political elements totally foreign to God's divine plan in Scripture. So, what do we do? We add Robert's Rules of Order, parliamentary procedures, votes, elections, bylaws, policy-based governance, meetings, more meetings, quorums, committees, and volunteers. There is no hint of any of these approaches in the New Testament.

These elements pollute, weigh down, distort, complicate, and subjugate the powerful mission of the divine *organism* called church. These elements become viewed as "baptized" and "sacred" over time: "We've always done it this way."

However, Christians have not always done it this way. In fact, the New Testament record, the biblical model, never did it that way—not even close! New, fresh expressions of biblical faith often start out in a biblical model. Yet, the human tendency for control creeps in over time. It's a tough spiritual discipline to let Jesus be the head of the church.

You might wonder, "How do well-meaning Christians—even some of those who write books about 'church governance'—drift so far from the biblical model?" Perhaps it is because there is no one chapter in the New Testament that focuses on biblical decision-making. It is not easy to grasp all the parts and pieces of a biblical approach to the ministry of leadership for the local church.

A few decades ago, God called me away from my favorite area of ministry: pastoring a local church. Since I had advanced training on a doctoral level, in both theology and missiology, the churches I served grew—even in challenging circumstances. God called me to start a ministry that would help other churches. In the process, I have seen so many churches that are plateaued or declining.

After working with 1,800 churches from seventy-eight different denominational and nondenominational families, it occurred to me: There is a major roadblock that has not been adequately addressed. It is the church decision-making process, often called church governance. It shackles so many churches—and denominations—from maximizing outreach effectiveness, to make disciples. Most of the common approaches to church governance actually hinder what God's people are called to accomplish. Politics cripples Kingdom work.

For two decades, I worked on an in-depth study of church governance. I started by defining governance as *the systems and approaches churches use to make decisions and implement changes toward effective mission and ministry.* My learning environment included Scripture and the many churches I consulted. I also read every book I could find about church governance models and, in some cases, interviewed the authors. It took thirteen years before I was ready to help churches with this monumental roadblock. My objective was, and is, to help congregations remove governmental gridlock barriers that undermine the mission. The goal is to help God's people make effective decisions from a spiritual perspective. My research included several complete trips through the Scripture.

For the last twenty years, Church Doctor Ministries has worked with numerous congregations from various denominational backgrounds and some independent churches. In the first five years, we continually refined the implementation process.

In truth? What we recommend sounds so radically different—at first! However, when congregational leaders and members learn biblical principles and then form a governance approach that fits the unique personality of their church, most everyone has the same response: "Why in the world did we do it the other way?" They are liberated. When the chains of bureaucracy are removed, the body of Christ impacts the world more effectively.

How do churches get stuck? The answer to that question has several parts: (1) Governance systems are inherited and rarely questioned. (2) Most denominational hierarchies and bureaucracies are formed in similar ways. So, it must be biblical—and good, right? (3) It is human nature for people to take control—even of God's movement. Of course, this concept is good for many aspects of life. However, it does not fit the unique, divine organism, the church of Jesus Christ. Jesus is the head of His Body, the church. He is supposed to be in control. Don't we believe and confess that? Isn't that what we have in mind when we call Him "Lord"?

In the New Testament, there is no name for this biblically based decision-making approach for the Christian church. It is simply assumed and demonstrated. While this is not typical for an *organization*, it adds to the evidence that Christianity is a *movement*. It is designed—by God—to move. In an attempt to help Christians grasp the scriptural culture of decision-making, I use two words that reflect the key *biblical* concepts of church governance. These concepts are nonnegotiable. The *form* they take can vary within the context of each congregation. Why? Each church, each body of Christ, has its own personality.[3]

Church governance, according to the Bible, can be described as an *apostolic theocracy*. This terminology can be easily unpacked and understood. Start with the second term: "theocracy." *A theocracy technically means "the rule of God."* All Christians confess and teach that we want what God wants. God is supposed to be in charge. This is usually described as "the will of God." As Christians, we want to do God's will—whatever it is that God wants. It is a basic element of the Christian faith. In the prayer Jesus taught His followers, we pray to God: "Your will be done, here on earth, as it is in heaven." For all decision-making in the body of Christ, doing God's will should be the basic standard for decision-making. God's will is the *end objective* for all Christians.

The word "apostolic" describes *how* we go about learning, seeking, concluding, and implementing God's will. Jesus modeled this, and the apostles practiced it in the early church. The approach in the early church was not toward building an organization. There were no votes. There was no majority rule. The apostles were focused on the will of God by what they learned from Jesus. The Lord frequently said, "The Kingdom of God is like...." Christ-followers constantly processed this in the young, emerging churches. Yet, the *apostolic* issue is this: How did they deliver this Kingdom of God culture? *They influenced through relationships*. No bylaws, no rules, no cookie-cutter organization. Instead, the focus was on teaching, coaching, encouraging, praying, and modeling. The focus was not on elections, but discipling. The operational approach was *not* focused on organizational bureaucracy, but moved forward by *relational influence.*

The apostles and local pastors of the movement, and the congregations, approached each decision-making conversation as a part of the larger universal organism. They operated as movement guides, not board members. Jesus didn't organize the disciples by using parliamentary procedures. He relationally discipled them. Paul's relationship to young Timothy was not defined by title, but by relationship. Too simple for today's sophisticated churches? Not according to those who have tried it!

The church, or groups of churches—like denominational networks—were never intended to be organizationally structured. The church is not a "pure democracy" where everyone gets a vote. Decisions are made by seeking God's will, through Scripture and prayer. Apostolic leaders influenced the general direction by pointing to the teaching of Jesus. In time, churches had the scriptural record, which we now call the Bible. Through prayer and the guidance of Scripture, apostolic leaders continue to influence others through relationships.

We have worked on revamping governance structures with many different churches and some denominations. The greatest obstacle faced by almost everyone is this: It sounds too simple! Ironically, it is just the opposite! It takes leaders who are committed to the will of God, according to Scripture. Therefore, it requires leaders who are lifelong students of Scripture. It represents leaders who pray, not vote; who seek consensus, not majority. It takes believers who practice followership. Leaders disciple other leaders who are committed to seeking God's will. There are no nominations, no elections. If this sounds wildly transformational—or foreign—it reflects how far Christians have drifted from the New Testament model for decision-making.

So, this is not normal, in the worldview of most Christians and churches today. Of course, God's church is supposed to be different. It is *very* different—or should be. Jesus made it clear: "My Kingdom is not of this world."[4] This is the "divine tension" experienced by every follower of Jesus: "in the world, not like the world."

So, we begin with the end in mind. How easy is it for a church to get back to a biblical form of church governance? To be honest, it takes some biblical paradigm shifts. There are always concerns about how it will work. However, with proper coaching, the change is always effective. Why? It is God's will. How do churches adapt and return to a scriptural form of decision-making? They are guided to use biblical principles to create a decision-making form that fits their unique body of Christ. The result? We hear this comment from every church where they have developed a biblical approach to governance: "We are liberated in the decision-making process!"

CHAPTER ONE

Church Alive!

People drift toward a bureaucratic organization. In Scripture, the church is a living organism.

Jesus: "And I will pray the Father, and he will give you another Counselor, to be with you for ever, even the Spirit of truth, whom the world cannot receive, because it neither sees him nor knows him; you know him, for he dwells with you, and will be in you."

—John 14:16-17 (Revised Standard Version)

- Have you ever gone home after a church meeting so upset you couldn't sleep?
- Have you sat in a meeting and quietly thought, "This is going on and on. Will it ever end?"
- Have you left a congregational meeting with negative—even unchristian—thoughts about one of your fellow church members?

- ☐ Do you feel frustrated and discouraged about your church and the lack of impact it has on your community?
- ☐ Has the decision-making process at your church ever made you feel like "there must be a better way to do church"?
- ☐ Do you ever feel like your denomination has drifted toward political gridlock?

Before you can consider anything about a spiritual decision-making process, look at your own congregation from God's perspective. You will find that perspective in the Scripture, particularly in the New Testament. Church is so unique, so unusual, so special—it is in a category all by itself.

Comprehending "church" often requires a paradigm shift. Jesus said, "My kingdom is not of this world."[1] The church is not anything like this world—at least, according to the Bible. However, the way we do church? Not quite the same, especially in the way we make decisions.

What is this entity called *church*? Is it simply another religious group? Is it just another multistep program? Is it primarily another organization? Or is it a movement? Is it a living organism? One thing is clear: The church is not that simple to define. Why? Many who profess to be part of a church describe it differently, based on their behavior. This reality demonstrates the confusion about what the church is, what it is not, or what it should be.

There are many ways Scripture describes the gathering of Christ-followers. The word "church" is only one term of many. Yet, it is the one most commonly used. The concept has followed a path into modern English—through Greek, Latin, and German.

The concept of church comes from the Greek New Testament word *ekklesia*. Technically, it means "those called out," implying that "church" is very different from other groups. It is unusual. It is special. It is unique.

The study of what it means to be "church" is called "ecclesiology." The primary source is the New Testament. The Scripture uses a number of metaphors to describe this unique entity. In summary, the church is a collection of people who are followers of, and believers in, Jesus Christ. It is clear that this organism called "church" is no ordinary organization. That should make church governance unique. There is no other entity quite like it. There are several biblical descriptions that help describe who we are and how we *do church*. The way we make decisions as church is called *church governance*. However, don't think of "governance" like "government." Think of it as decision-making. Think about it as seeking God's will—and doing it. Think of it as following Jesus.

"Church" is no ordinary organization.

THE BRIDE OF CHRIST

The New Testament describes the church as *the bride of Christ*. A bride is not a building, an institution, a platform for programs, a place to go to, or a dead museum of old-fashioned antique rituals. This bride is a living, beautiful organism, loved by Jesus—the Groom: instinctively, unconditionally, with high expectations to be fruitful and multiply offspring. The process of developing offspring is called "making disciples" of Jesus Christ.

"Membership" to a bride is like a marriage license. It is just a piece of paper. It is the relationship that counts. It is intimate and personal. Being in such a relationship with the King of the universe is very special. It is described as being *faithful*.

As Christians, we are in an intimate relationship with the bride. We don't really "join" a church. We don't "go" to church. We don't actually "belong" to a church. We *are* church, by marriage!

We *are* church, by marriage!

SHEEP OF THE SHEPHERD

The people of God are the *sheep of the Shepherd.* Sheep aren't the most brilliant of animals. They easily wander off. On their own, they get lost. They are vulnerable to forces that would destroy them, especially if they are alone.

So, God puts people together. They are protected in the flock—called "church." They grow close to the Shepherd, who would lay down His life to protect them. He is a Good Shepherd—really good!

The flock is a relational gathering: Sheep are connected to each other and connected with the Shepherd. It is not an organization of independent entities. There is no organizational chart, no hierarchy among sheep. Church is a community in protection, with strength in numbers and with the guidance of the Good Shepherd.

Sheep don't vote on where they go. They look to the Shepherd for guidance. They follow the Shepherd, who would rather die than see one lost. This is the group dynamic for those who trust the One who guides their lives.

> **Sheep don't vote on where they go.**

THE TEMPLE OF GOD

The followers of Jesus are described in Scripture as the *temple of God.* Yet, this is no ordinary building. It is not an institution. Institutions come and go. Buildings eventually fall apart.

Not this building! This is the temple of the living God. The Scripture says that God's people are living stones. Jesus is the cornerstone: the key, defining part of the building.

The living temple is dynamic. The structure where the living stones gather is temporary. Christians are building blocks. Christ still lives in this world. How? He lives in people. When the people are scattered and the structure is empty, the real church penetrates the community.

...the real church penetrates the community.

This building is a living organism: fluid, dynamic, and impactful. It is empowered by God. The living stones are ignited by the resurrected and living cornerstone—Christ. "Building the Kingdom" isn't constructing a monument. It is introducing and developing spiritual life in others. There are no organizational blueprints. The living stones impact others who become more living stones for the King of the universe, Jesus. He has His stones constantly involved in a building project.

THE HOUSEHOLD OF GOD

In the New Testament, the church is described as *the household of God*. Families don't vote. Good parents don't ask their children to help them decide whether they would rather pay the mortgage or go to Disney World.

Healthy families develop relationships of influence. They don't hold meetings and cast ballots. Parents don't develop bylaws for their kids. While they do have guidelines for behavior, their modeling, like discipling, influences behavior more than anything else.

Most people would agree: "Family comes first." The church is not a bureaucracy of stakeholders. From the perspective of Scripture, it is a close-knit family of relationships—with Jesus and also with one another.

The glue that works in families is not politics, but relationships of influence. The power of influence for the church is in the relationships with Jesus and with other Christians. The family represents a slice of the Kingdom of

The church is not a bureaucracy of stakeholders.

God. Kingdom culture reflects the values, beliefs, attitudes, priorities, and worldviews of the King.[2]

The greatest impact for productivity is not a download from the constitution, a purpose statement, or a vision document. It is mission culture, which is more caught than taught. The household of faith is not a corporate mechanism with rules and regulations. It is a family where the children catch values from their parents at the dinner table. The family doesn't need bylaws—just values.

A ROYAL PRIESTHOOD

The Scripture describes God's people as a royal priesthood. The followers of Jesus are not volunteers. They become different people, reborn. God doesn't *use* people. Jesus honors people by inviting them to come along on the transformational journey of a lifetime.

The Holy Spirit gives spiritual gifts to Christ-followers. These gifts are not the individual's choice. They are not the organization's agenda. They are the divine design of God Himself. At baptism, you were ordained to ministry.

> **God doesn't *use* people.**

The church is not an organization of boards, committees, offices, and titles. No one "runs for office" and, depending on the vote count, wins—or loses. No one loses in this Kingdom. Jesus has no bylaws for losing, but enormous compassion for the lost. Everyone belongs on His team. Every person, each with unique gifts, is on a mission from God. No one sits on the bench.

The church is a living, breathing, dynamic organism. Your gifts determine your "sweet spot" of ministry. You are not elected to anything. Everyone is part of the elect. You are called. You don't have a job. You have a mission. When you find your calling, church is not an organization that needs

> **No one loses in this Kingdom.**

your help to function. Church becomes an organism where you discover divine direction. No one "works for the church." You are in partnership with the Ruler of the universe. You are valued. You report to Him. He died for you so you could live for Him. You are a minister. Every believer is in ministry.

THE BODY OF CHRIST

The church is the *body of Christ*. The church is not just any Body. It is not another organization. For anyone who is a believer, it is not an optional opportunity to "get involved." It is a divine, supernatural privilege.

The church is the Body of Jesus Himself. He is the Head of His Body. The Head controls the Body. The Head shapes the direction, sets the pace, chooses the priorities. The pastor is not the head of the Body. Neither is a board, a team, or a staff.

The function of leadership is to focus entirely on the supernatural direction set by the Head—and communicate that direction to all the living parts of the Body. The mission isn't determined by the leaders. The leaders are determined by their commitment to the Head, their clarity of the mission, and their gifts, given by the Spirit.

The work of the congregation is not determined by a budget. The budget is determined by the calling of the Head. Since the Head is perfect, the direction—the will of the Head—trumps everything else. The priorities of the Head are clear: "Seek and save the lost" and "make disciples." The direction of the church is not left to the influence of George or Jane, a board, or the latest program.

Denominational leaders don't set the theme and direction for your church. Leaders ask God for direction. They ask, "How can our church most effectively reach lost people for Jesus?"

The only guidebook available for the body of Christ is Scripture. The more people know this book, the better off the

Body will be. The mission is demonstrated by the Head. The more people know Him, the more productive the Body will be. God's people need fewer bylaws and more Bible. Naysayers say, "That is too simplistic." They represent confusion about the role of law and the power of the Gospel.

In the next chapter, we will look at a brief history of how inherited governance structures have come into being. We will discover how we have received forms of decision-making that are *foreign* to Scripture. It will become clear that we have often developed systems that are influenced by secular approaches rather than by God.

Reflective Questions for Chapter One: Church Alive!

1. Why do you think there are so many metaphors about the church in the New Testament? What do they tell you about the *nature* of the church?

2. What do all the descriptions of the church say about the *function* of the church?

3. Do you normally think of your church as a "living organism"? What does that mean to you?

4. Church governance reflects "who's in charge." What do the descriptions of "church" in the Bible demonstrate about how decisions should be made?

Reflective Questions for Chapter One: Church Alive!

CHAPTER TWO

But We've Always Done It That Way!

Religious people perpetuate rituals; Jesus' movement is contextually adaptable.

"You guide me with your counsel, and afterward you will take me into glory."

— Psalm 73:24 (New International Version)

It is amazing how bad ideas can be handed down among Christians for so long they seem spiritually right, even most productive. What is really surprising—and disturbing—is how many believers simply accept approaches that are counterproductive to the health, vitality, and growth of the local church.

In this chapter, we look at a brief history of church governance structures. *The infusion of secular influence is as evident as the absence of scriptural support.* You may not be convinced about this reality simply by reading this book. However, if you put Bible-based approaches into practice in your church, you will feel empowered for mission and ministry. Your church will become more productive. That is an absolute fact! Let "Scripture alone" be your guide. That is a Reformation principle worth applying to your church. It liberated thousands of churches from bureaucratic shackles. Your church can be freed from legalistic, political tyranny.

How do I know this? We have worked with numerous churches from many denominational and movement backgrounds, guiding leaders to develop a biblically based governance approach that works for the unique personality of each congregation.[1]

It is clear from Scripture that the enemy who tempted Jesus in the wilderness is hard at work among faithful people in churches. The Scripture describes him as a "roaring lion." He is also a cunning bureaucrat! Secular politics and human forms of church governance are subtle but powerful roadblocks to the primary mission Jesus gave to His followers. Honestly, it seems so easy to drift toward high control and so hard to leave it in the hands of Jesus. This is a spiritual issue!

Removing secular forms of church governance is not a "silver bullet" to increase your congregation's ability to reach lost people in your community. It will, however, remove roadblocks that sap energy and frustrate God's people. It will free you to be the church that Jesus intended. You will be more prepared to be missionaries to your own social networks and your community. Removing the weight of non-biblical church governance allows your church to become healthier. When churches are healthy, they are powerful. Healthy congregations impact their communities. Healthy Christians change the world.

It seems so easy to drift toward high control.

Historically, there are several bad choices churches could make as a platform for decision-making. Each of these approaches is influenced by secular culture. As we look at the different forms, consider your own church's decision-making process. If your congregation is part of a denomination, think about the approaches used by the larger church body. If you become like others who have gone through this process, you will likely wonder, "Why in the world would we *do church* that way?"

"Why in the world would we *do church* that way?"

There are seven dominant forms of church governance. Many churches follow some sort of combination of the different forms.

#1 HIERARCHY

The Old Testament approach of hierarchy is based on the high priest model. This is a vertical structure for church governance. In the Old Testament, only the high priest could enter the holy of holies.

At the time of Jesus, the Jews were still following this model. You may remember, when Jesus was arrested, they led him to Caiaphas, the high priest at the time. This hierarchical model reflects leaders who are called "congregational presidents," "regional bishops," "district presidents," "conference superintendents," among other titles.

The Roman Catholic and Eastern Orthodox churches primarily operate from a hierarchical model. In the United Kingdom, the King is the figurehead of the Church of England, though the Archbishop of Canterbury is the one who represents the church in Parliament.

Some nondenominational, charismatic, Pentecostal, and independent churches follow a local version of this model. In these congregations, the senior pastor is in charge of all decisions and the direction of ministry. In some cases, the lead pastor is called a "bishop" or "overseer."

Some emerging Christian movements have governance approaches that are hierarchical. In the grassroots movements of Africa, for example, many people are led by a village "chief." This form moves over into growing churches. However, as these churches mature, many of them move beyond the hierarchical model to use other forms of church governance.

#2 DEMOCRACY

At the other extreme of the hierarchical model are those churches that follow and operate as a "pure democracy." In the history of Christianity in the United States, the first churches in the British colonies were Anglican.

However, with the arrival of the Puritans, many of the emerging congregations were patterned after pure democracies. Every member helped decide everything. From this approach emerged the congregational form of church governance.

In the extreme congregational form, anyone in the church can call a meeting about any subject, including the removal of the pastor. Everyone gets a vote. The majority rules. Several years ago, I was invited to consult a declining church in an urban setting in Pennsylvania. The pastor was a gifted leader. Their form of government was extreme congregational. About a year later, one member of the church rallied members to demand a vote on the future of the pastor. They got just enough votes to remove the pastor. One day he had a calling to ministry, and the next day he had no job! He went down the road a few miles and started a new church. It became the largest church in the area. The previous church eventually died. For some reason, they had difficulty attracting another pastor!

#3 REPUBLIC

By necessity, many churches with congregational forms of government moved on to a system that seemed more practical. In the evolution from congregational to republic forms of decision-making, a smaller group would be chosen to make decisions for the rest.

In the republic form of governance, many churches have adopted the political system of their nation. Nominations are sought, votes are taken, and those elected are chosen to represent the rest of the congregation.

In this system, those nominated are often leaders in the business community or those who are well known within the church. They are, in most churches, not vetted on their knowledge of Scripture. Further, in the voting approach, most churches require at least one other person to run *against* the other. After all, this process with only one candidate would reflect influence from the hierarchical approach. Consequently, there is a "winner" and a "loser." This raises an interesting question: Why would a person willing to serve God ever be labeled a "loser" in front of their church family? How does that fit in the culture of the Kingdom?

In the republic form of governance, candidates are often chosen without knowledge of their spiritual gifts, which is a scriptural value. Rarely in this approach does anyone reflect on the spiritual maturity of those "running" for a position in the election. Even less often are political candidates asked about their understanding concerning the primary purpose of the church.

#4 DEMOCRACY/REPUBLIC MIX

In this form, there is a mixture between republic and congregational forms of church governance. From the republic side, there are nominations and elections. Leaders end up in a decision-making group, which can operate under many different titles: consistory, elders, deacons, church council, board of directors, and many others.

However, on issues of "great importance"—which range from changes in the worship schedule to anything that requires the use of money—the group must bring it to the whole congregation for a vote. This part of the process is a remnant of the democracy model.

One consequence of this approach is that after leaders have worked diligently on a decision, they must bring it to the congregation. They are required to explain how and why they arrived at the issue proposed. They are required to take questions. Meanwhile, the meeting drags on and on. If the larger group votes to decline the proposal, there are several results. The "leaders" aren't really leading. Further, the leaders are discouraged. The meetings run longer. Eventually attendance declines. Meanwhile, the church struggles to get a "quorum," another concept totally foreign to Scripture. Throughout this process, new Christians ("baby" Christians of any physical age) are encouraged to vote and direct the future of the church. As a result, fewer members see any value in serving as a "leader." This would include those who are most qualified—*gifted* leaders who wouldn't want to "waste" their time.

#5 OLIGARCHY

This form of governance occurs when long-standing individuals or families are dominant within the congregation. This is common in small churches. Since the majority of congregations are smaller (200 or fewer in attendance), the oligarchy may be the most prominent form of decision-making in the Christian movement.

The oligarchy is ***not*** constitutional in these churches. In other words, regardless of what form of governance is mentioned in the church constitution, in *reality* the church operates as an oligarchy.

The dominant people or families in an oligarchy influence—by numbers, and occasionally by intimidation—the rest of the church, including the pastor and staff.

This also occurs when a very wealthy or well-known person from the community is an active part of the church. They have the power to hijack the direction of the church through their influence. Perhaps they are seen as leaders because of their wealth, status, or dominant personalities. In some churches, someone who is seen as a community leader—such as the mayor—is considered a good leader for the church. However, a civic leader may be limited in scriptural knowledge and the wisdom of God. That leader may only show up at church for Christmas, Easter, and congregational meetings. This is one of several issues that hold churches back from breaking what is called the "200 barrier," or 200 or fewer people in worship. The oligarchy reflects a power struggle in the church, and it can last for decades—or generations of a dominant family.

#6 COEQUAL PLURAL ELDERSHIP

In this form of church governance, the church is led by coequal leaders that often include the staff—or at least the pastor. In this approach, there is, in reality, a "corporate pastor" represented by a group. The group includes the pastor or pastors and may include some staff, along with elected or chosen leaders from the congregation.

In some churches, they are called "elders," and in others they are called "deacons." Some churches identify this group as a "church council" or "executive board." Other congregations may call them "trustees."

In Presbyterian churches, for example, this group is called the "Session." Among Presbyterians, this structure is a core definition that dominates the denomination. In other words, their decision-making structure defines them more than biblical doctrine or mission priorities. However, many Presbyterian churches—while faithful to the structure as the defining element—have redefined their ministry and vision in line with mission priorities. This is especially true of the more conservative Presbyterian congregations that have left their former denominational structures.

The coequal leadership can result in undermining the role of the pastor. At the other extreme, the coequal eldership raises the ministry influence of those who are non-staff elders.

#7 THEOCRACY

The word "theocracy" means "the rule of God." In churches that follow this model, the most visual priority is a form of church governance driven by a strong and overarching desire to identify the will of God from Scripture.

Most leaders in all these models will say they are primarily interested in the will of God. However, in practice, their priorities are occasionally demonstrated through personal agendas. In other theocratic forms of governance, the priority for God's will is genuine. There is a strong and overarching desire to identify the will of God. In these churches, leaders bring their Bibles to a decision-making meeting and search Scripture for discussions that move toward a consensus to direct the church.

The theocracy form recognizes, in theology *and* practice, that Jesus Christ is the Head of the church. From that position, decision-making responsibilities are shifted from the congregation to those who are identified as God-ordained *leaders*, without diminishing the involvement of the priesthood of all believers, who are primarily equipped and involved in *ministry*. By definition, congregational members are busy doing ministry and are therefore not involved in leadership. Leaders are chosen by their lifestyle of Bible study and their commitment to Scripture as the authority for direction. These leaders disciple the next generation of leaders. Usually, but not always, those who lead in the theocracy model have the spiritual gift of leadership. However, the commitment to scriptural guidance is nonnegotiable.

#8 APOSTOLIC THEOCRACY

An apostolic theocracy combines the commitment to God's will, through Scripture, with the approach of a nonvoting, nondebating, nonpolitical, anti-high-control-oriented atmosphere. Decisions are made at the leadership level by consensus, through Bible study and prayer. In the following chapter, this approach will be described in detail as the most biblical and effective model for church governance.

Reflective Questions for Chapter Two: But We've Always Done It That Way!

1. What is the difference between a "religion" and a spiritual movement?

2. Have you been frustrated or angered during a church meeting? Did you ever feel the *approach* to making decisions leads to frustrations?

3. As you read about the different forms of church governance, which one most closely reflects the approach to decision-making used at your church?

4. How often do you make decisions based on the Word of God?

CHAPTER THREE

Apostolic Theocracy: Organizational Control or Movement?

People drift toward control; Christ rules His church.

"I will instruct you and teach you in the way you should go; I will counsel you with my loving eye on you."

— Psalm 32:8 (New International Version)

In the last chapter, we looked at the major categories or types of church governance used around the world. In many cases, the approaches are more reflective of a human design than of the New Testament church.

In recent history, particularly since the Protestant Reformation, churches have followed two general models for organizing. The Roman Catholic and Eastern Orthodox streams of Christianity have followed the *hierarchical model* of the high priest, an Old Testament model used before the birth of the Christian church at Pentecost.

In many European churches, this model has focused on monarchs. Kings and queens, for hundreds of years, were the local "heads" of the church. This is the top-down *political* model. In this context, Robert's Rules of Order were "baptized" as sacred in many areas of Christianity.[1] Parliamentary procedures were elevated as if they represented Scripture. Can you imagine the Trinity requiring a two-thirds vote? Could you see the disciples or Apostle Paul "calling the question"?

MODELS FOR MOVEMENT

Building on these models, the many approaches to the operational side of the church have been shaped by business, corporate, and governmental models. Congregations—and whole denominations—have adapted both structure and constitutional approaches that actually diminish the movement dynamic of the New Testament church.

These organizational approaches have many negative ramifications for the church. For example, the position of "pastor" has drifted significantly from the scriptural model. The clergy are subtly relegated to the position of "employee." This results in an emphasis on professionalism or what might be called clericalism. In Scripture, service in the Kingdom of God is a calling. From the human perspective, it may feel "scary" to allow the Holy Spirit to guide every Christian into service, equipping each one with spiritual gifts. It seems logical—though not biblical—to form a "board of control." Welcome to the *organization* that undermines the movement.

This scenario can be seen in many churches. After the worship service, there is a scheduled luncheon for a special event. Before the meal begins, a layperson approaches the pastor and says, "It's time to start. Please pray so we can eat." It seems like a small issue. However, it represents a style and approach to ministry. When it is repeated, the church takes yet another organizational step toward diminishing the movement power that God intends. Any Christian can pray!

The concept of discipling, as Jesus modeled, lifts the church from an organization to a movement. Pastors model discipleship multiplication, as Jesus demonstrated. Yet, the movement never ends with the pastor, staff, or leadership. The discipleship multiplication occurs throughout the church. It occurs as parents disciple their children. The discipleship lifestyle multiplies the movement.

Years ago, when I served as the pastor of a church in Detroit, I trained members to be involved in ministry. They discovered their spiritual gifts and were trained in various types of ministry, according to those gifts. One of those areas was hospital ministry. Members were equipped through the process of "on-the-job" discipling, just like in the New Testament. However, when they visited some members, the frequent response was, "Where is the pastor?"

We have programmed generations of Christians in an organizational model. However, in Ephesians 4:11-12, the *movement multiplication model* is clear. God has given certain gifts to the church: apostles, prophets, evangelists, pastors, and teachers. Their purpose is "to equip God's people for the work of ministry." This is the multiplication model that leads toward a movement. Christianity moves exponentially. At least, that is God's plan!

We have programmed generations of Christians in an organizational model.

Jesus demonstrated the movement model. He spent the majority of His time equipping the twelve through "on-the-job" discipling. It follows six steps that lead to movement multiplication: (1) "Come, follow me"; (2) "I do/you watch"; (3) "I do/you help"; (4) "You do/I help"; (5) You do/I watch"; (6) "We both repeat this process, as an ongoing lifestyle."[2]

This discipling process leads to exponential growth. The organizational model leads to a maintenance mentality of organizational bureaucracy. This approach results in growth by addition. The movement approach results in multiplication. Addition turns the movement into a program. Multiplication gives birth to a movement.

> **Jesus demonstrated the movement model.**

CONTROL ISSUES

Denominational bureaucracies are magnets for control-oriented believers who have missed the biblical focus on the mission of the church. Most of them mean well, but miss the culture of the Kingdom. They lock Christians and churches into a system that handcuffs the Holy Spirit, who, like the wind, blows in directions human beings can't imagine.[3] The result is the enormous amount of time, money, and energy focused on political activities.

The believers who suffer the most from the gridlock of bureaucracy are often those who are mission-minded. They tend to ignore politically charged meetings filled with debates and votes. They are more excited by the New Testament Acts of the Apostles than by Robert's Rules of Order.[4] They would rather learn how to reach lost people than become experts on bylaws.

Over time, denominations operated by enthusiastic bureaucrats stall in effectiveness. Their corporate culture fails to attract the most gifted leaders focused on mission. Whole denominations become bogged down in politics. Meanwhile, those in the rank and file who are politically enthusiastic are drawn to denominational leadership. Inevitably, the political machine loses the vision for the primary mission of Christianity, simply by neglect. Controversial agendas infiltrate the denominational culture. Those with mission passion vote with their feet. Individuals join other churches. Whole congregations disengage from their historic denominations. They feel liberated from the "political machine." They begin the journey toward mission, unhindered or distracted by the corporate drift of their previous organized structure. They are liberated for mission.

The organizational model for church governance is usually focused on control, which is a good idea with many benefits. The question is: "*Who* is in control?" In a faith movement, God is in control—or should be. The centerpiece of the Christian faith is God. God is in charge. That is what Christians confess.

The church was birthed on Pentecost with the power of the Holy Spirit. Christians believe that. Yet, when it comes to operational approaches, human beings slip into self-control mode. This is a faith issue. We believe God for salvation, but subconsciously retreat when it comes to the operational church. We opt for boards, bylaws, and bureaucracy to organize—control—the church. The movement is robbed of its divine power and replaced by programs we can control.

In a faith movement, God is in control—or should be.

The Protestant Reformation was a great step forward for the body of Christ. Basically, Christians got back to the Bible, a return from abuses in previous centuries. Yet, it was not much to take the next step: from biblical control of doctrine to organizational control, which puts the Holy Spirit in handcuffs.

The way some local churches are organized, they become the ideal place for those with a control mentality. Control-oriented people gravitate to places of power in organization-oriented congregations. When they get to the level of power—a board or an office—they can do enormous damage to the church. They are not bad people. They are victims of a political environment that has drifted from Scripture. When believers develop a control platform, they provide a political playground. It is a magnet for control freaks. It is clear from the New Testament that the church grew by being out of (human) control. That scares some people, but delights the Holy Spirit!

Control-oriented bureaucrats are often oblivious to biblical ecclesiology—the teaching in Scripture about the uniqueness of the church. They are the prime instigators of frustration for pastors, staff, and other Christ-followers who clearly understand the dynamics of the New Testament approach to church. The greatest champions for the Great Commission suffer at the hands of control-oriented bureaucrats in the church.

When good leaders are frustrated by controlling people, the central issue is always the basic biblical view of the church as a living organism (movement), versus a bureaucratic organizational worldview. This situation not only frustrates the best mission-minded church workers, but it also causes a downward spiral of effectiveness for the church and an upward spiral of discouragement for the pastors, staff, and those who understand the biblical model—and who have a passion for the Great Commission.

The church, operated as an organization, is the ideal landing site for people with narcissistic personality disorder. By the nature of this mental illness, churches that lean toward, or allow, control orientation provide the ideal destination for narcissists. The preoccupation of a narcissist is control. Often, the narcissist is not consciously aware of their disorder. In a church with a control approach to organization—as well as the propensity of Christians to forgive and tolerate—narcissists find the perfect climate. They can destroy churches. In our work as Church Doctors, we see this often. Since pastors and church leaders know a lot about mercy, but not much concerning narcissistic personality disorder, this abusive behavior disrupts many congregations.

MOVEMENT THROUGH APOSTOLIC THEOCRACY

The church of the New Testament movement is based on the teaching of Jesus and the apostles. It is a *theocracy*—focused on what God wants. This model becomes clear by carefully studying the Christian movement in the New Testament. First Peter 4:1-2 says, "Since Jesus went through everything you're going through and more, learn to think like Him. Think of your sufferings as a weaning from that old sinful habit of always expecting to get your own way. Then you will be able to live out your days free to pursue what God wants instead of being tyrannized by what you want."[5]

In a theocracy, Christians take seriously the fact that Jesus Christ is the Head of His Body, the church. Spiritually mature leaders are identified, discipled, and chosen, not nominated or elected. They are Christians who exhibit a lifestyle of Bible study. They represent a passion for studying God's Word. They are more interested in biblical truth than in human bylaws or "the way we've always done it."

The church of the New Testament is a *theocracy*.

These leaders are usually a small group—regardless of the size of the church. Jesus chose twelve. Our experience reflects that the ideal size of a leadership group should be six to twelve people, depending on the size of the congregation. The approach to decision-making is more important than the number of leaders. When they meet, they bring their Bibles. On issues discussed, they tap the wisdom of Scripture. They want what God wants—and this is their general approach to every decision.

They support their pastor, who is called by God to lead the decision-making group and the church. The pastor follows Proverbs 15:22, "Without counsel plans go wrong, but with many advisers they succeed."[6] The pastor seeks wisdom from the group, whose members operate as Bible-influenced counselors. These leaders are characterized by their humility and willingness to listen to anyone in the church, one-on-one (not in meetings), anyone who has insight for the direction of the church. This approach recognizes that God can reveal His will to any Christian.

However, input is funneled through the leadership counsel.[7] Scripture is the lens of authority.

THE WORD "APOSTOLIC" IN SCRIPTURE

The tone of this biblical approach to governance is *apostolic*. The apostles were selected, not elected. They were recognized by the fruit of the Spirit. The origin of this concept includes two sources. The first is the behavior and approach of the apostles in the New Testament. Second, they were spiritually minded, yet not political.

To be clear, there was one instance when they "voted." It was to fill the spot vacated by Judas. In Acts 1:20, Peter spoke publicly, quoting Psalm 109:8, that someone should take the place of Judas. He said it should be someone who witnessed Jesus' resurrection and was part of the larger group of His followers (Acts 1:21-22).

The disciples offered two candidates to replace Judas: Barsabbas, who was also known as Justus, and Matthias (Acts 1:23). Then they prayed for God's guidance. That was a good idea! However, in Acts 1:26, they drew lots to see which one would "win." Matthias got the position, which brought the team back to a total of twelve apostles. Notice: This was a vote—a political move.

Interestingly, we never hear from Matthias again! It's like he disappeared from Scripture. However, by Acts 6, the Christian movement was growing. The young "church" was expanding. The apostles needed help. Instead of drawing lots, the Scripture says, they asked their group to "choose seven men among you who are known to be full of the Holy Spirit and wisdom.... The group presented them to the apostles, who prayed and placed their hands on them" (Acts 6:3-6). The end result? "And so the word of God continued to spread. The number of disciples in Jerusalem grew larger and larger..." (Acts 6:7).

But what about the twelfth apostle? In Acts 9:1-25, the persecutor, Saul, meets Jesus on the road to Damascus. Saul was chosen, not elected. No votes! Saul was recruited by Jesus. When Saul went to Jerusalem and tried to join the other apostles, they would not believe he was a changed man. However, Barnabas spoke on his behalf. Saul then began preaching in the name of the Lord. Saul chose to go by Paul, his Roman name. Paul was chosen, not elected. The end result? Acts 9:31: "Through the help of the Holy Spirit, (the church) was strengthened and grew in numbers...." Paul became an apostle.

The word "apostle"—in the context of an "apostolic theocracy"—is a form of church governance based on Scripture. Scholars define "apostle" as "one sent with a special message or commission." In other words, they are "sent people," outward looking—focused on the mission. They are not primarily focused on the basic task of "housekeeping" or regulating the church. They are not charged with the priority of running the church "decently and in order."

The word "apostolic" implies authority. The title "apostle" in Scripture reflects a "commissioned" messenger or ambassador. Ambassadors are chosen, not elected politicians. They are leaders in a co-mission, in partnership with Christ and His church.

In the first generation of the early church, the word "apostle" represents (1) a church leader and (2) one who is qualified as a "missionary." A missionary is technically "one who is on the mission of the Gospel." The concept of "apostle" reflects someone Jesus "sends out"—with a view toward outreach and a passion for growing the church. An apostle has the authority of Jesus to focus on continuing and extending His mission for the salvation of others.

THE OPERATIONAL APPROACH OF APOSTLES

The second reason we use the word "apostolic" for biblical governance is based on how the apostles operated in the New Testament. They didn't form government structures. They didn't debate. There was no hint of a quorum. They were not political.

Instead, their lifestyle reflected a commitment to Jesus. They were consumed by efforts to reach others for Christ. Their decisions were based on His teachings and the Old Testament. They were filled with the Holy Spirit. Their primary posture was spiritual.

The apostles were in stark contrast to most of the religious leaders—the scribes and the Pharisees. They were "enthusiastic"—a word translated as "those filled with God." Their tone was all about love and compassion. They were prayer warriors. Their primary objective was to reach people for Jesus.

The apostles had a variety of spiritual gifts. They weren't all evangelists. Only some of the apostles had the gift of missionary, the calling to reach out to others cross-culturally. They were empowered by the Holy Spirit and eager to do whatever it took to help the local church reach the world for Jesus.

The apostles were people of prayer. They looked for guidance from God's Word. They spent time and energy on their top priority: to reach people for Jesus. They didn't influence others with rules and regulations, laws and bylaws. They led people to (1) experience Jesus, (2) build His church, and (3) reach those who were not yet believers.

When the apostles gathered together, their "meetings" were brief, and their passion was to seek God's will. Their work was to multiply Christ-followers and take the Gospel to the ends of the Earth.

Apostolic leaders chosen for governance in your church should be those who reflect "...love, joy, peace, patience, kindness, goodness, faithfulness, gentleness, and self-control."[8] They will also have a passion for mission: to go, make disciples (Matthew 28:19-20), and be witnesses of Christ (Acts 1:8).

Apostolic leaders place high value on and commit to the commandment to honor one's father and mother. This commandment reflects that as Christians we respect all who are in authority and honor our leaders.

The biblical approach to governance is *apostolic.*

Who would be an example of this type of leadership? Study the character and leadership dynamics of Jesus, the Apostle Paul, or Peter. Look at great leaders who influenced the Christian movement in history: St. Ignatius, Martin Luther, John Wesley, Billy Graham, and others.

An apostolic theocracy serves the church as a flat decision-making team. It is characterized as servant leadership. The pastor is the leader of leaders, as was Moses.[9] There are no votes, except required by civil law. There are no congregational meetings for decision-making, no quorums or simple majorities. The apostolic leaders make decisions by consensus, not votes. Decisions follow prayer and Bible study, which influences discussion. There is no debate, only discussion. The leaders approach all decisions in the same manner as the New Testament leaders did: "It seemed good to the Holy Spirit and to us...."[10] They seek God's counsel. Consequently, this leadership team is identified as an *apostolic counsel.*

Apostolic leadership occurs through relationships.

Many churches have a decision-making group called a "church council." In the book of Acts, it was the Pharisees who occasionally met in a "council," which reflects their religious, politically charged focus on Old Testament law. When the Christians met, Acts calls it a "counsel." This reflects a priority for seeking counsel from God and Scripture rather than by means of debate and votes. The difference for the culture of leadership is huge! (This topic will be unpacked further in Chapter Five.)

Apostolic leaders will continually look for and pray for—until they find—someone who appears qualified and ready to be discipled (not elected) to become a future leader. As leaders leave the *apostolic counsel,* they are replaced by those they have discipled, on the job, at leadership counsel events.

In the next chapter, we will look at all the peripheral dynamics and teachings that surround church decision-making.

Reflective Questions for Chapter Three: Apostolic Theocracy: Organizational Control or Movement?

1. This chapter reveals the drift toward control. Some aspects of our world could make us feel like we are not in control. Do you think that could influence Christians to overcontrol our churches?

2. Throughout Scripture, the people of God often had no control over their world. Consider the Israelites as slaves in Egypt or when the Romans occupied Israel at the time of Jesus. Do challenges influence Christians to take control at church or in denominations?

3. Have you thought about your faith—and your church—as a movement? How does your church reflect the spontaneous multiplication of the church in the New Testament?

4. In the Lord's Prayer, Jesus models an approach to seek God's direction. We pray: "Your will be done, on earth, as it is in heaven." When you reflect on how you and your church make decisions, is that your approach?

CHAPTER FOUR

Developing a Leadership Team

Some churches get buried in bylaws; spiritual leaders follow Scripture.

"...I did not shrink from declaring to you the whole counsel of God."

—Acts 20:27 (Revised Standard Version)

Bill was watching one of his favorite television shows with his wife when the phone rang. He checked his caller ID. It was Paul, a leader at church.

"Hello," Bill answered.

"Hey, Bill, it's Paul, from church. I hope I'm not interrupting you."

"...No, Paul, that's OK," said Bill, as he walked from the living room to the kitchen. "What's up?"

"Yeah, Bill, ah, well, I was asked to serve on the nominating committee for our upcoming election at church." Paul paused. "And, well, our constitution says we need at least two names on the ballot for each position. Anyway, I was wondering if you would let me put your name up for vice president of the congregation."

Bill paused as his mind raced through a short list of ramifications. "Well, ah, I don't know, Paul. Isn't Mary currently in that position? Has her term ended?" he asked.

"No, she can be reelected. And I think she may be willing to continue," Paul responded, "but the constitution requires two names for each position."

Bill silently thought, "But what if she doesn't run again?" Finally, he broke the silence. "I don't know, Paul...I'm not sure I'm qualified...ah, I'm not sure I could do that job," Bill shared, as his mind raced.

"Oh, you'd be fine, Bill," Paul replied, then paused. "Yeah, the council meets only once a month, and I'm not sure, but I think they skip July and August—and maybe December." Paul thought for a minute, then continued, "What do you say, Bill? It's really hard to find people who are willing to serve. Can I put your name in?"

"Yeah, I guess so," Bill said, as he felt a nervous twinge in his stomach.

• • •

The more you learn about Scripture and see how most congregations operate, the more you wonder, "How on earth did the people of God drift so far?"

Think about Bill. If he wins the election, he has no idea, really, what he's getting into. And Paul has no clue if Bill is even spiritually qualified. In fact, Paul has never learned about his own spiritual gifts. Bill hasn't, either. In truth, the position of vice president of the council has a one-line "job description," with no mention of qualifications, except "member in good standing," which in some congregations means you are not dead!

If Bill loses, how does that help him? Why should Bill, or anyone in a congregation who is willing to serve, lose—publicly—

in front of all their friends and fellow members of the church family? In the spiritual realm, wouldn't God want everyone to be a *winner*—every individual involved in service to God? How is this approach even remotely related to Scripture?

STRUCTURES OF CHURCH GOVERNANCE

As a Church Doctor consultant, I've had the opportunity to meet with nearly two thousand decision-making groups in congregations. There are numerous forms and approaches to leadership. There are church councils, elders, sessions, consistories, boards of lay ministry, deacons, boards of directors, and many others.

The names of these governance mechanisms are less important than the way they function. Most of these approaches are patterned after secular organizations. They are flavored with church language, but the basic approaches of most churches are borrowed from the world, not influenced by the Bible.

Why? Part of the reason is that there is no chapter in Scripture that provides a spiritual approach to decision-making. However, if you dig deep enough and look far enough, Scripture provides everything you need to know about making decisions in the body of Christ.

You won't find a sample, cut-and-paste constitution in the Bible. But the principles of decision-making are clear, and they are everywhere. And, after helping dozens of churches—of various sizes and backgrounds—retool to a biblical form of church governance, there is ample evidence that it works. In fact, the impact is phenomenal. Church leaders—and entire congregations—are liberated for maximum effectiveness. Who wouldn't want that?

> **Scripture provides everything you need to know about making decisions.**

Is the biblical model for decision-making perfect? Yes, from the perspective of Scripture. No, from the perspective of human beings! Why? People are subject to corruption. Nevertheless, following God's plan and approach empowers God's people to do God's work in God's way.

Many forms of church governance are sprinkled with nuances of the Old Testament, where the law is central. Under the new covenant, the New Testament provides refreshing approaches to decision-making. They are gospel-oriented. They are grace-infused. Once a church makes the change, the people will never go back to the old approach. In fact, the most frequent question is, "Where did that old governance structure come from in the first place?"

Many of the historical approaches draw examples from the world. In the age of monarchies, many churches bought into the heavy-handed, top-down, high-control approaches to decision-making. This has led, in some areas of Christianity, to layers of bureaucracy filled with rules and regulations and bylaws by the billions! At the denominational level, the rules and regulations are multiplied! Surprise! Parliamentary procedure is not found in the Bible.

In more recent years, many dimensions of the Christian movement have been strongly flavored by corporate business management models. These approaches and others are adapted from the world. They are foreign to the movement launched by the God of the Scripture. They roadblock the movement potential of congregations. Secular forms represent a substantial roadblock to the effectiveness of the Christian movement. They tend to reshape the church. They move the church from a dynamic organism to a static organization, from grace to law, from spiritual power to political gridlock.

As mentioned in Chapter One, the Christian church, described by numerous metaphors in the New Testament, is a living organism. This makes the church unique—and very different from an organization. When the organism is treated like an organization, it turns the movement into a program, a multilayered bureaucracy. This corruption extinguishes the explosive potential for multiplication that Jesus built into the Kingdom of God. Instead of exponential growth, the church, at best, grows by addition. An unbiblical governance model is one of Christianity's major roadblocks.

THE KINGDOM OF GOD

Jesus arrived on the Jewish scene, as predicted. He was a Jew among the Jewish people. Most of the Jewish religious leaders couldn't handle the movement Jesus started. This New Testament form, this new testimony God revealed, went right over the heads of most of the religious leaders—even though their own prophets pointed to it!

> **An unbiblical governance model is one of Christianity's major roadblocks.**

The religious leaders had a hard time dealing with Jesus because He brought a new paradigm. In the New Testament, Jesus was asked by Pilate if He was King of the Jews. It was a political question. Jesus responded, "My kingdom...doesn't consist of what you see around you."[1] The way the Kingdom works is not supposed to be like this world. However, many believers, it seems, struggle with radical change—even if it is much better!

Matthew, writing to the Jews, called it the Kingdom of heaven. Even then, most of the religious leaders didn't get it. The scribes and the Pharisees were stuck in their ways. They were politicians of religion. In effect, the religious hierarchy said, "We've always done it this way."

To fully experience the liberation brought by the biblical paradigm of church governance, you will need to help people in your church refresh a New Testament philosophy of ministry. This is an operational approach to what Scripture says about church and decision-making. The New Testament form of governance is very different.

A biblical philosophy of ministry is based on Scripture.[2] The Bible is the only guidebook Christians have for operating the church. One of the greatest challenges Christians face is the political practice of voting. Is voting really a "church thing"?

VOTING IN THE CHURCH

There are no references to voting mentioned in the New Testament, except for two instances. Acts chapter 26 is the account of the Apostle Paul pleading for his life before King Agrippa. He explained that when he was a Pharisee, he was against Jesus of Nazareth. He admitted that, in Jerusalem, he jailed many followers of Jesus, by the authority of the chief priests. He said, "...when they (the followers of Jesus) were sentenced to death, I also *voted* against them" (emphasis mine).[3] He went on to explain that this was before his Damascus road experience. In all of Paul's letters in the New Testament there is no mention of Paul voting or recommending to the churches that they vote. Once Paul joined Jesus' movement, he left politics behind. We should as well!

The second reference to what may be described as a "vote" occurred early in the young Christian movement. In Acts 1:16, Peter spoke to 120 people not long after the resurrection of Jesus. He announced publicly that Judas had betrayed Jesus and was now dead. In Acts 1:21-23 (as mentioned in Chapter Three), Peter announces a replacement for Judas. During the ministry of Jesus with the twelve disciples, there were many other men and women who followed the Lord. They experienced, firsthand, the teaching and activities of His work. Peter goes on to explain that the group of eleven disciples put two names forward for the position left by Judas. One of the men was Joseph, called Barsabbas, who was surnamed Justus. The other was Matthias. In verse 24, Peter tells the crowd how the disciples made the choice between the two men. They prayed (verses 24-25), and they "cast lots," sometimes translated "drew straws." Matthias "won," and in Acts 1:26 it says, "...he was enrolled with the eleven apostles."

When looking at church governance, some Christians see the reference about Matthias as a biblical approval for voting. For example, it is common practice for churches to place two names on a "ballot" for one position, requiring church members to choose the "winner." On further study, however, the *context* of Scripture supports, if anything, that this was not the right approach for filling the spot left by Judas. Why? (1) This is the only reference to Matthias in the New Testament. You never hear about him again! (2) Jesus Himself appointed the twelfth man, Paul, on the road to Damascus (Acts 9:1-22). (3) Nowhere in the New Testament is there any hint that decision-making includes votes. With all the advice given to the churches throughout the New Testament, by the Apostle Paul and others, not once is there an instruction to vote. This is further understood by the meaning of the word "apostle."

The use of the term "apostle" represents a person who is "commissioned." They are chosen, not elected. Apostles are "messengers" or "ambassadors." These are not political concepts. "Apostles" are co-missioned—marked as a "missionary" of the gospel movement. They are focused on the mission to spread the good news of Jesus Christ. Bible scholars identify apostleship as a purely religious commission to carry out the purposes of God for the salvation of people. It is a lifelong authorization, given once for life.

The designation of "apostle" has *normally* been restricted to those in the New Testament era. However, the word "apostolic" refers to the manner in which the apostles guided the church. This has great implications for anyone who leads anything in the church. In Ephesians 4:11-12, the concept of apostle is listed as one of the "equipping gifts." It is an area of ministry that equips *others* in the church for the work of ministry, according to their gifts. This "equipping gift" is listed alongside "prophets, evangelists, pastors and teachers." Those "equipping gifts" are not additions to the original twelve apostles, but *functional* gifts that continue in church ministry roles. They are gifts of the Holy Spirit. They are not sought by the individual. They are discovered, like all the gifts of the Spirit.

New Testament churches do not elect people for ministry. Instead, ministry leaders help all Christians discover, develop, and use the gifts of the Holy Spirit—the spiritual gifts God has given to each of them.[4] The word "apostle" when used *outside* of the New Testament does not describe an office, like the original twelve, but a function, like the other gifts of the Holy Spirit.

APOSTOLIC THEOCRACY: WHAT DOES IT LOOK LIKE?

In Matthew 6:10, Jesus teaches us to pray. In what has become known as "The Lord's Prayer," Jesus says, "...your will be done, on earth as it is in heaven." In Matthew 7:17-20, Jesus speaks about "bearing good fruit." He follows by saying, "Not everyone who says to me, 'Lord, Lord,' will enter the kingdom of heaven, but only the one who does the will of my Father who is in heaven" (verse 21, NIV).

An apostolic theocracy form of church governance is based on biblical approaches to decision-making. Again, the word "theocracy" means: "We want what God wants. We want to do God's will." This is a statement of faith that directs local church leaders toward a biblical approach to decision-making. This commitment toward church governance is first and foremost. Those who make decisions for the congregation are chosen, not elected. They are chosen from among those who demonstrate deep knowledge of Scripture and a lifestyle of personal and group Bible study. They are not "newcomers" to the Word of God and the ministry of the church. They are mature in biblical wisdom. It is not a "job" or "office." This unique area of ministry is their *calling*.

There are no votes, no term limits. Those in leadership serve until God calls them elsewhere. When they meet, they are led by the pastor. They never meet without their Bibles. They refer to

Scripture for direction. They frequently pause the meeting for prayer, whenever it is needed. They always work toward reaching unanimous consensus in which no one objects to the decision or questions the outcome. If they can't reach unanimous consensus, they table the issue. Their focus is entirely on following God's will. The skeptic will say, "This could lead to *decision gridlock*." From that biblical perspective, it refers to "perhaps it's not God's timing—let's table it and pray about it." "Maybe it isn't what God wants," or perhaps "we don't have all the right people around the table who focus entirely on God's Word."

An apostolic theocracy is based on biblical approaches to decision-making.

Jesus calls all Christians to "make disciples." Those who are called and chosen to serve on an apostolic decision-making team will disciple their replacements. They will continually look for and pray for—until they find—an apostolically gifted member of the church who will be added, by consensus, as a *disciple* of the member who called them to serve. The discipler will mentor (disciple) the person into this apostolic ministry.

In the next chapter, we will look at the nature and function of this form of church governance. We will take a closer look at the concept of theocracy and describe the difference between the two structures: a council or a counsel.

Those who are called to serve will disciple their replacements.

Reflective Questions for Chapter Four: Developing a Leadership Team

1. Have you ever been asked to be nominated to a position at your church? In that process, did the person ask you about your spiritual gifts? Did they urge you to pray about the position?

2. Have you ever questioned the governance mechanisms at your church? Have you wondered about their origin? Did you consider whether they reflect Scripture?

3. How do you make decisions? Whether they are small or large issues, do you pray, read Scripture, and/or seek guidance from another mature believer? When you pray the Lord's Prayer and say, "Your will be done," do you consciously focus on your life, church, and family?

4. Perhaps you have helped at church or volunteered at some ministry in your community. Did you reflect whether God has *called* you to serve in that area? Are your efforts in line with the spiritual gifts the Holy Spirit has uniquely given to you?

CHAPTER FIVE

Council or Counsel?

Boards are guided by constitutions; Christians are led by the Scripture.

"For to us a child is born, to us a son is given, and the government will be on his shoulders. And he will be called Wonderful Counselor, Mighty God, Everlasting Father, Prince of Peace."

— Isaiah 9:6 (New International Version)

When individuals are chosen by popularity, they reflect the will of the masses. To identify the will of the crowd, people vote. The entire process is political. It gives birth to rules and regulations, laws and bylaws. Jesus warned the disciples, "...beware of men, for they will deliver you up to councils...."[1] I don't think Jesus was talking about church councils, though the concept might fit in many congregations!

Biblical Christians are supposed to live by the will of God. They will "...seek first his kingdom and his righteousness...."[2] They pray "...your will be done...."[3] These concepts are not political, but spiritual. They give birth to grace and power, joy and fulfillment.

The form of church governance you pursue will determine the culture in which you make decisions. That culture will influence the philosophy of ministry of those in your church and those your church attracts to leadership positions.

Biblical Christians live by the will of God.

CHOOSING YOUR CULTURE

When Jesus introduced the Kingdom of God, He lost the support of many of the religious leaders from His Jewish background. He lost them. They killed Him, but only temporarily. The Jewish movement, somewhere along the line, moved from *spiritual* to *religious*.

Religion prioritizes the forms, the practices—all the stuff you do around church. Religion can be your servant—a medium to perform and celebrate your faith. It can also grow, subconsciously, to become your master. It can become a false god—a tyrant that controls and takes center stage of your life and the life of your church.

The Jewish movement moved from *spiritual* to *religious.*

Faith is trust in God, a relationship with Christ, a hunger to grow, to serve, to worship, to pray. It is powered by the Holy Spirit, using your spiritual gifts—your unique, spiritual DNA to be a disciple who makes disciples, grows the Kingdom, and changes the world.

Religion loves rules and regulations, procedures and bureaucracy. It is a control mechanism. It forms habits that have long lost their original meaning and usefulness. It blossoms into political power. It is transferred to people in corrupted forms, in archaic, "feel-good" approaches that inhibit the effectiveness and the growth of God's Kingdom. Church people become *irrelevant* to those Jesus wants them to reach. The Jesus movement gets stalled. It is roadblocked by His own people.

The culture of the Kingdom is not like this world. It is dramatically different. It really does take faith to believe it is your best choice for life and for your church. Kingdom culture is not the clothes you wear or the buildings you construct. Jesus impacts your worldview. You see the world differently. *Nothing looks the same through the eyes of faith in Jesus.*

Jesus warned, "...My kingship is not of this world...."[4] Why? His people—like you and me—are in this world, but by faith, we go beyond the ways of this world. We confess that we want what God wants. We want to do His will. We even pray, "...your will be done...."[5] It is not about what I want or what you want. It is not even what the "majority" wants.

This makes the practice of the Christian faith dicey. Yet, when we rise above all that pulls us away from His Kingdom, we experience Jesus. It is life on a whole new level, a higher level. It includes a constant battle. The world is always pulling us in other directions. Yet, though we are in the fight, Christ has already won the victory. It really makes sense to follow Jesus.

The culture of the Kingdom is not like this world.

It is in this complexity that we gather as *church*—a community of believers called *ekklesia*, which means "that which belongs to the Lord." The church is called out—called away from the world, yet stationed in the world. Church is a community gathered by God through Christ. We are the people of God, not *of* the world, but *in* the world. We are continually and simultaneously *called* out of the world and sent back into the world.

As church, we must make decisions. The church is "unique." It is not a democracy. The people in church do not have absolute power. The power for decisions is in Christ. Christ is the Head of His Body called church. He is "the brains of the outfit."

Making decisions in the church amounts to seeking the will of the Head. That is neither easy nor simple. Many of the challenges we face in everyday church life are not covered directly in the Scripture. Christ rules the church through His Spirit. That means decision-making is a spiritual exercise. *Church governance is the spiritual discipline of discernment.* This reality impacts every facet of how God's people go about making decisions in their church. Clarifying the biblical and spiritual nature of church decisions is a prerequisite for every step of developing a decision-making approach for your congregation.

Church governance is the spiritual discipline of discernment.

THE PHARISEES AND THEIR COUNCILS

Many churches have "church councils." Most congregations that call their decision-making mechanism something different operate within a similar culture. If you are nominated, elected, and vote, your form of church governance is *political.*

These forms of church governance are so common, most believers simply accept them as "the way we do church." The important question is, "Are they biblical?" If that question reflects, "Are they in the Bible?" the answer is emphatically "Yes!" "Are they politically charged?" Absolutely! "Are they God's approach?" Absolutely not!

The decision-making entity called a "council" in the New Testament is the product of the world—the political world! Jesus tells His disciples, "...beware of men, for they will deliver you up to councils...."[6]

It is the Pharisees—the *religious* leaders—who are connected to councils. The Scripture reports, "Now the chief priests and the whole council were seeking false testimony against Jesus that they might put Him to death...."[7] This is a blatant reference to religious politics.

In Acts 5:21, Peter and John were caught in a political drama: "Now when the high priest came, and those who were with him, they called together the council, all the senate of the people of Israel, and sent to the prison to have them brought." In verses 27-28, the Book of Acts reports, "...they set them before the council. And the high priest questioned them, saying, 'We strictly charged you not to teach in this (Jesus') name....'"[8]

Later in Acts 5, the political, dictatorial and proud Pharisees are challenged by one of their own: "a Pharisee in the council named Gamaliel" said, "So in the present case I tell you, keep away from these men and let them alone, for if this plan or this undertaking is of man, it will fail; but if it is of God, you will not be able to overthrow them. You might even be found opposing God!"[9]

In this reference, some of the Pharisees reflected a *control-oriented*, political approach. However, Gamaliel turned the *council* culture into a *counsel*-oriented approach. The basis for his advice? "...if it is of God." He took the political atmosphere and turned it into a spiritually based discussion. See the difference? A *council* is a political, human-centered approach. A *counsel* is an approach that seeks direction from God.

THE COUNSEL APPROACH

In Acts 20, the Apostle Paul speaks to the elders in Ephesus. His spiritual approach focuses on God, not on rules, traditions, or politics. Paul says, "...for I did not shrink from declaring to you the whole *counsel* of God."[10]

A *counsel* is an approach that seeks direction from God.

In his letter to the Ephesians, Paul writes a statement that captures the unique culture of spiritually led decision-making. He says: "In him, according to the purpose of him who accomplishes all things according to the *counsel of his will*...."[11]

These forms of church governance, council and counsel, are two distinct, diametrically opposite approaches to church governance. The church council concept is most often tied to religion, control, and political maneuvering. Yet, the approach of a church *counsel* looks to the wisdom of God. The cultural ethos is not politics or votes. It is seeking the wisdom of the Lord. It is not constitution-centered but Scripture-centered. It is not vote-driven but prayer-driven.

COUNCIL OR COUNSEL?

This is not simply a matter of semantics. The two approaches are totally different. They represent two divergent philosophies of ministry. The council approach is more popular in churches and denominations today—no question about it. However, the counsel approach is faith-based. It has been tested in many churches. It reshapes the atmosphere.

Why? There are two reasons: (1) The *council* approach is bureaucratic, which does not fit a living organism like the body of Christ, the church. Politics divide. A council tempts participants to focus on human approaches. (2) The *counsel* concept is Scripture-driven, not constitution-centered. The source is God, not human corporate thinking. God serves as our *counselor.* Scripture is our *counsel.* Leaders (1) seek God's counsel and then (2) counsel the church to follow God's direction, based on Scripture. This biblical modeling by leaders is powerful and contagious. It reshapes the health and potential of the church.

To unpack this important aspect of church governance, it is helpful to look at the meaning of these two ideas. They are not simply words. They are concepts that are antithetically different. Getting this right makes a huge difference in the effectiveness of your church.

The first thing the Merriam-Webster dictionary notes is that *the words council and counsel are often confused in form and meaning.* This may describe the governance challenge facing local congregations and denominational structures. A "council" is described as "a group of people called together for consultation, discussion, and advice." Notice that the advice comes from the people, not God, not the Word of God. At this level of definition, there are only slight difficulties.

However, the word "council" is further unpacked in the Merriam-Webster dictionary as "a group of people chosen as an *administrative, advisory*, or *legislative* assembly." This is where a church drifts toward a political organization. It is the beginning of nominations, votes, term limits, extended constitutions, bylaws, and Robert's Rules of Order. The more you study Scripture, the more you realize the distance in culture between the council concept and the biblical model based on the teaching of Jesus and the apostles.

No matter what your church or denomination calls the decision-making group, there are several challenges when you govern from the perspective of the council. *The challenge with "administrative"*: Whether you call your decision-making group a board of directors, church council, session, consistory, elders, or whatever, in the world of the church, most leadership groups meet only monthly. Some meet less often. "Administration" requires "on duty," everyday attention, or at least most days. When "administrative" duties are relegated to a decision-making group that meets once a month, the process becomes weak, uninformed, and, perhaps most important, impractical. Administration is an everyday task, or at least five out of seven days a week.

The difficulty with "advisory": Groups that only offer advice rarely impact the direction of the larger body. When people are elected to a leadership group, most issues are more complex. In addition, each leader advises from his or her own life and work experience. It is dangerous to restrict advice for the uniquely and divinely designed Christian church to each person's experiences from the workplace.

The problem with "legislative": Votes focus on the will of the majority rather than the will of God. Many church meetings with a legislative perspective will include those who have strong personalities, but may be weak in the biblical wisdom of God. This is, perhaps, the most dangerous, difficult, and disastrous occurrence in churches. Those who are asked to serve in a decision-making position of the church are rarely vetted through the lens of their Bible knowledge, frequency of Bible reading, Bible study, or their personal commitment to scriptural truth. Based on real-life experience, most seasoned pastors and biblically mature members would agree.

A church with a "legislative" *council* is prone to be money-centric. We've seen this challenge in many churches. You've probably heard the phrase "almighty dollar." If money rules, you have a secular god. Of course, fiscal responsibility is appropriate for the church. But as a driving force, it turns the spiritual movement into a secular business. Too often, churches have large endowments, but declining membership. Frequently, that is a sign of misplaced priorities. The church is not a bank.

At the other extreme, some churchgoers' favorite mantra is "we can't afford it." Instead, think of it this way: "If it's God's will, it's God's bill." In other words, God pays for what He orders. Too many churches have more money in the bank and fewer people in the church. In Acts 8:18-24, Peter encountered a guy named Simon, a man who thought Christianity was all about money. He offered money to the apostles so he could receive the Holy Spirit. Peter responded, "May your money perish with you, because you thought you could buy the gift of God with money!"[12]

THE COUNSEL OF GOD

The word *counsel* is described by the Merriam-Webster dictionary as "a mutual exchange of ideas, opinions, discussion and deliberation." In the church, the ideas and opinions are formed by Scripture. The word "counsel" is, of course, related to the idea of "consultant." Did you ever look at Jesus' teaching and training of the disciples as a form of consulting—as well as discipling? Have you ever considered the letters of Paul to the churches as a dynamic of consulting? The Scripture, the Word of God, is the central theme of the Protestant Reformation. The reformers sought to strengthen the Christian movement through *sola scriptura*, Scripture alone. Scripture counsels believers. Believers counsel one another. Leaders counsel the direction and decisions for the church. Their source is Scripture alone. The word *counsel* in Scripture reflects the *plan* and the *purpose* of God.[13]

THE COUNSELOR HAS COME

From the word counsel, we receive the personification: counselor. In Isaiah, it says, "For to us a child is born, to us a son is given; and the government shall be upon his shoulder, and his name shall be called Wonderful *Counselor*, Mighty God, Everlasting Father, Prince of Peace."[14]

Jesus says, "If you love me, you will keep my commands. And I will ask the Father, and he will give you another *Counselor* to be with you forever. He is the Spirit of truth...."[15]

Those who guide a local church—or a group of churches—are to take counsel from *the* Counselor, the Holy Spirit, through the Word of God—Scripture. They call on the Holy Spirit for guidance as they seek the wisdom of God. They are not bureaucrats or politicians. They operate apostolically: in relationship to Christ, relating through the power of the Gospel to those in the church.

At Church Doctor Ministries, we advise churches to form a leadership team as an *apostolic counsel* and develop a decision-making process that models an apostolic theocracy. These concepts will be the focus of the next chapter.

Reflective Questions for Chapter Five: Council or Counsel?

1. Churches have different names for their decision-making groups. What does your church call that group? Do you know how it functions? Is it primarily political or prayerful? Is it driven by the Scripture or bylaws? Are those who are chosen to serve in the decision-making process qualified by a willingness to serve or on the basis of God's will?

2. Have you asked yourself, "Am I more spiritual or religious?" How do you understand the difference?

3. In your church, when big decisions are made, is the focus on what God wants or on what the majority decides?

4. The religious Pharisees were out to stop the movement launched by Jesus. They held political *councils*—votes and debates. The Christians gathered for *counsel*—searching the Scripture and praying for direction from God. How does your church operate? What about your family? How do you make important, personal decisions? Do you regularly ask the Counselor, the Holy Spirit, for help (John 14:15-17)?

CHAPTER SIX

Appointing *Apostolic Counsel* Members

In most churches, leaders are elected by votes. In Scripture, leaders have a calling.

"I bless the Lord who gives me counsel...."

— Psalm 16:7a (Revised Standard Version)

In the last chapter, we focused on the difference between a church council and a church counsel. Based on the biblical, New Testament model, a counsel has the Kingdom culture of the Counselor. It is not political: Members are not elected, but chosen. It is a calling, not a "position," "job," or "office." They are discipled on the job—an approach described in the next chapter. They are led by the (senior) pastor. Their guide for counsel operation is not a constitution, but Scripture. Perhaps most important, counsel members are qualified by their lifestyle, reflecting commitment to and involvement in Bible study. They are students of Scripture. They have spent years in group Bible studies or taught Sunday school. They have a lifestyle of regular, personal Bible study.

GOD'S WILL

In the Lord's Prayer, we pray, in so many words: "We want Your will—what You want, Lord—here on earth, in our lives, in our church, just as it is in heaven."[1] Those who serve on an *apostolic counsel* are committed to seek God's will through scriptural truth. The Bible is the source and norm for all discussions. The climate is shaped by conversations like, "It seems to me that, according to Scripture, God would have us pursue...." With that comment, it would be likely that the person may turn to the chapter and verse and a discussion of interpretation would follow. You would never hear, "Well, I think...," or, "At our former church, we...," or, "According to the bylaws...."

During discussions, an *apostolic counsel* could pause for prayer on a regular basis. There would also be times when there would be a pause to search the Scriptures, with discussion following. There would be an overarching priority to know the will of God, to "...seek first his kingdom...."[2] In the context of the mission of the church, just as the Father sent Jesus, we are sent by Jesus to reach the world for Him.[3]

The counsel is apostolic. There are no votes or approaches in which the "majority rules." Everything is decided by consensus, reaching the level of "one mind." In 1 Corinthians 1:10, Paul writes, "I appeal to you, brethren, by the name of our Lord Jesus Christ, that all of you agree and that there be no dissensions among you, but that you be united in the same mind and the same judgment."[4] When the issue seems clear, the leader, the pastor, asks the counsel members, "Does anyone object?" If no one objects, the issue has been addressed. There are never votes. If the issue doesn't reach total consensus, the discussion continues. Lack of consensus will move the group to prayer. It may also include Scripture-based discussions. If there is still no consensus, it is tabled for another time, with the understanding that *God's timing* may not be "right now." This is an apostolic theocracy. We are asking God to speak to us: personally, through His Scripture, in prayer, in our hearts, or later, if necessary.

At this point, you may quietly hear a little voice in your head: "Are you kidding me? That will never work. We will never decide anything. You can't run a church that way. You'd never lead a denomination like that. Nothing would get done!" Tell that voice to listen to Scripture. Those who have tried this biblical approach have learned two lessons: (1) Scripture is always right, and (2) it's great to be liberated for effective ministry. They have also learned, with people involved, nothing is always perfect. Yet, God uses people anyway!

WHAT ARE THE OTHER QUALIFICATIONS?

When you begin to identify those who could serve on an *apostolic counsel,* you may find very few who demonstrate—by their Bible study lifestyle—that they are "ready." Or, you may find that there are many who have spent years in God's Word, but may need to grow in biblical understanding at a leadership level.

Further, your leadership team should consist of those who are genuinely humble. If someone says they are "proud" to be a leader, that could reflect false pride. Servant leaders are not ego-driven, but mission-focused. Remember the words of John the Baptist? When asked about his position in relation to Jesus, he said, "He must become greater; I must become less."[5]

It may sound strange, but after working with many churches in the process of developing *apostolic counsels,* I would *not* have chosen myself, just after I graduated from seminary! Oh, I spent hundreds of hours in the Bible during my four years at Christian college and four years of seminary—even with one of those years as an intern in a church. Of course, I spent many hours in Scripture when I was in school. I even learned to translate the Hebrew of the Old Testament and the Greek of the New Testament. The real issue? Most of my training was in an *academic* context. I had not spent much time in Scripture wrestling with the many challenges of life and the challenges of a congregation.

Consequently, *apostolic counsel* members should be those who are mature in the faith as well as familiar with the depth of Scripture. If you end up with only three Christians on the counsel, that's fine. Remember, you don't have a preconceived, mandated bylaw for a certain number of slots to fill. Your *apostolic counsel* will focus on quality biblical discussions. Pray. Ask God to direct you to those He has prepared and called.

SPIRITUAL GIFT MIX

Once you have determined to search for candidates who are called to serve on your *apostolic counsel*, work on developing an "ideal" team spiritual gift mix. What are the gifts of the Holy Spirit that should be represented on your decision-making team? From the spiritual posture of the New Testament, focus on spiritual gifts that you perceive to be nonnegotiable requirements for an *apostolic counsel.*

> ***Apostolic counsel* members should be mature in the faith.**

It may surprise you—and disappoint you—that in spite of the Scripture's focus on spiritual gifts, the vast majority of Christians have never discovered the unique gifts the Holy Spirit has given them. In Romans 12, 1 Corinthians 12, Ephesians 4, and a few other scattered references, the New Testament addresses the gifts of the Holy Spirit.

In Ephesians 4, the apostle addresses the "equipping gifts," sometimes called offices. As mentioned earlier, they include: apostles, prophets, evangelists, pastors, and teachers. What is their very important role? According to Ephesians 4:12, those gifted in these areas are to "equip all Christians to do the work of ministry."

One of the serious deficiencies in many churches is the culture of "staff" doing ministry and church members helping out as "volunteers." The concept of volunteers is foreign to Scripture. This will be discussed in a later chapter. When you discover your spiritual gift mix, you begin to find the ministry to which the Holy

Spirit has divinely and uniquely called you. Even in congregations with five hundred or more worshippers, it would be rare to find two people with an identical dominant and subordinate gift mix. Yet, it is safe to assume that somewhere among those in your congregation, God has supplied all the gifts you need to be an effective, healthy congregation that can accomplish everything God calls you to do.

As you move toward developing an *apostolic counsel,* those involved should be conversant with spiritual gifts teaching or be willing to learn. There are many spiritual gifts discovery tools based on Scripture. The candidates who qualify for your *apostolic counsel* may be known for their dominant and subordinate spiritual gifts. If that is not the case, the learning experience about spiritual gifts should be part of your selection process for the *apostolic counsel.*[6]

The concept of volunteers is foreign to Scripture.

The needs, challenges, and uniqueness of your congregation will also help determine the gift mix of each member of your *apostolic counsel,* as well as the overall gift mix of the group.

Some spiritual gifts are a part of the gift mix of most *apostolic counsels.* These gifts will include, but are not limited to, the following New Testament gifts of the Holy Spirit: leadership, wisdom, discernment, faith, intercession, apostle, administration, exhortation, and teaching.

To be clear, few Christians will have all these gifts. Further, some may have only a few of these among their dominant and subordinate gifts. What matters is that these gifts are included in the overall gift mix of the *apostolic counsel.*

THE NEW PARADIGM OF "COUNSEL"

You may call those on your congregation's *apostolic counsel* anything you choose, of course. It would be most helpful to resist political or organizational names, such as president, vice president, and others. The "leader" should be the (senior) pastor, as mentioned earlier.

Our use of "apostolic" counsel reflects the way in which New Testament apostles influenced the biblical direction of the young churches. They were not political or dictatorial. They sometimes reflected on their experience as well as their role as servants. However, the most common emphasis for influence was *relationships*. This included their relationship with God Himself. Even Paul, who was not one of the first disciples, established his connection with Jesus when it occurred on the road to Damascus. Why was he blinded? Perhaps it was a lesson in humility—another key factor for those who serve on an *apostolic counsel*. The apostolic leaders in Scripture were not elected. They were identified, called into ministry, and commissioned. The believers laid hands on them and prayed for them. Their calling was not to rule, but to serve.

Most often, the basis of the apostles' authority is their confession, their experience of faith, and their service to the Lord, as well as their relationship with those in each of the churches. In order to comprehend the real power of relationships, it is important to recognize what "church" was like in the New Testament.

The "church at Jerusalem" or at Ephesus or Galatia was not an established building or specific location. It was usually a cluster of house gatherings. The apostles frequently traveled. They discipled other travelers as the movement grew. This is the point: They did not relate to *organizations*. They exercised the power of relationships.

The apostles... exercised the power of relationships.

Likewise, your *apostolic counsel* will be focused on relationships: with the Lord, with each other, with the church staff, and with congregational members. This approach builds *relational influence*. It displaces political influence.

Why did this model work so well in the New Testament era? The first reason is that it is biblical. God demonstrated the value of a relationship: He showed up in Jesus, a real person to whom every believer can relate.

There is a second reason relational influence worked in the New Testament world. My favorite way of explaining it is simple: People did not have refrigerators! Consequently, they had to visit the marketplace every day, or at least regularly. The marketplace is where people got the local news. It was a way of life, a conduit for information. Relationships were the glue for community. In the marketplace, Christ-followers shared the good news about Jesus.

Today, our world has a different, but equally beneficial, platform: the Internet. In fact, it is called *social* media! You have a personal social network. In the New Testament, new, excited Christians "gossiped" the gospel to their social networks—those they met at the market. Your social network is those on the directory you carry in your phone. Your personal mission field is on a contact list in your pocket!

Highly organized and politically charged churches tend to develop "programs" that are often building-centered. They reflect *organization*. A movement—like a revival, or a spiritual renewal, or a reformation—is powered through relationships. This approach turns an organization inside out. Why? Leaders influence. A "board of directors" or "church council," or any political entity, emphasizes *organization*. A relational, called, chosen, nonvoting, praying, Scripture-discerning group changes the paradigm to relational influence. It establishes a paradigm shift for your church. It triggers a *movement*.

Your personal mission field is on a contact list in your pocket!

This approach would have the same impact on whole denominations locked in political gridlock. These larger forms of church governance are eventually ignored by their constituent congregations and/or politically self-destruct as whole groups of churches leave. What is the posture of these churches that step out of the denominational malaise? They are liberated! And, they are highly relational.

LEGAL REQUIREMENTS

Since congregations are located within political entities—states, provinces, countries—there are always a few nonnegotiable "constitutional" issues. The New Testament clearly reminds believers to respect government leaders. In those areas, it will require a "political approach of voting." It is a tension churches have had from the beginning: Reduce the politics to an absolute minimum while maintaining respect for the government and the laws of the land.

The New Testament church became an explosive movement. Maximize the power of relationships. Minimize the politics. Vote only when the law requires. Diminish the length of the constitution. Focus on Scripture, operate through spiritual gifts, and function on the platform of relationships.

When votes are legally required, you can approach those decisions in a way that is more biblical. If you operate with an *apostolic counsel*, allow those members to present the biblical criteria for the vote. Seek to move toward consensus to whatever degree possible. Instead of asking, "All in favor?" say, "On this biblical basis, does anybody spiritually object?" Even when you must vote, use it as a teaching opportunity to reflect Scripture-based decision-making.

Reduce the politics to an absolute minimum.

HOW MANY?

When we work with churches to develop a better form of church governance, the "mundane" issues seem to surface early in the process. One of the most common questions early on is,

"How many should serve on the *apostolic counsel*?" Perhaps you have already had this question cross your mind. It's hard to move from a democracy paradigm, where everyone is in charge, or from a republic approach, where elected leaders are responsible. It is an additional challenge to move toward a theocracy, where God calls all the shots. It is easier to explain to the six-year-old Sunday school class than the sixty-year-old member of the church. Yet, we are called the "children of God" for a reason!

First, there are some theological guidelines for the size of your *apostolic counsel*. Whatever the size, you want to focus on where God is working, moving, and blessing. This is one way to demonstrate that you are willing to let God be in charge. That means no nominations, arm-twisting, recruiting, or votes to pick those who serve on the *apostolic counsel*. Instead, consider: Who is known for their commitment to Scripture? Who shows that commitment? There is a caution: Don't confuse religious commitment ("the way we've always done it") with universal truths of Scripture.

Second, don't worry too much about the size of the counsel. There are large churches that have only four or five "counselors." Further, remember, each of them should be constantly looking for, and praying for, someone with similar commitment to a life in Scripture who would benefit from being *discipled* by a counselor. If you have four counselors on your *apostolic counsel*, as well as the pastor as a leader, and each of the counselors is discipling another, that would be nine people in the room. Even though "disciples" will not normally be involved in the discussions, you probably don't want more than six counselors, plus the pastor as leader, plus six observant, silent disciples.

As a next-level approach to accountability, we recommend churches use external professionals to assist and guide them with financial audits and other important stewardship and financial decisions.

In the next chapter, we will look at the role of discipling. While it might seem obvious to Christians, our practice shows that the vast majority of believers are not aware of the basic elements of discipleship multiplication, which leads to the rapid expansion of the Christian movement. This is surprising, since Jesus gave the marching orders: "Go, make disciples," as a fundamental approach. We will look at that next.

Reflective Questions for Chapter Six: Appointing *Apostolic Counsel* Members

1. This chapter reflects the biblical approach called an "*apostolic counsel.*" For many, this is a new concept. Without going back to the chapter, can you describe from memory what each of those words mean, why they are helpful, and how they are biblically based? (If not, go back and review the first section of the chapter.)

2. The *apostolic counsel* approach requires a commitment to prayer. In the Lord's Prayer, Christians say they want God's will to be done, on earth, just as in heaven. Does this earnest prayer occur often among the leadership group in your church? Does it reflect a strong element of your life?

3. Leadership for ministry should seek God's will and unanimous consensus. Does this seem to be unrealistic? How do you understand this Scripture: "...that there be no dissensions among you, but that you be united in the same mind and the same judgment" (1 Corinthians 1:10)?

4. Christians want to make good decisions. Have you always made good decisions, even when you were young? Or, did you mature over time? What does that mean for those who make decisions for your church? How does a Christ-follower grow in biblical maturity? Does that process help you recognize who might serve well in the leadership of your church?

CHAPTER SEVEN

Jesus' Dynamic Approach

Churches beg, "Can we get a volunteer?" Jesus said, "Come follow me."

"In him, according to the purpose of him who accomplishes all things according to the counsel of his will, we who first hoped in Christ have been destined and appointed to live for the praise of his glory."

—Ephesians 1:11-12 (Revised Standard Version)

Not once did Jesus ask, "Can I get a volunteer?" In fact, the word "volunteer" is found nowhere in the New Testament. The concept is foreign to the Scripture altogether. Good decision-makers are discipled, not elected.

Yet, there are whole books published and devoted to developing a great "volunteer ministry" for your church. Actually, those two words, "volunteer ministry," taken together, are an oxymoron! In fact, the concept is repugnant to the culture of the Kingdom of God. If that sounds shocking to you, then you have just experienced a snapshot of how far many churches have drifted from Jesus' approach!

Technically, God doesn't "use people," in the popular sense, to continue and multiply His mission. The Lord has a much higher level of respect for those who are in partnership with Him, through the ministry of His church.

Not long ago, I was worshipping at a church we are consulting. Before the service began, there were several announcements scrolled on the screens. They included:

> "We need people to help with the coffee and refreshments used for fellowship after the service."
>
> "We need help in the office to prepare the worship folders."
>
> "We need more people to read the Scripture lessons for upcoming worship services."

This whole approach is foreign to the culture of the New Testament church. However, you wouldn't know that if you visited most congregations.

God *calls* people to join Him in the mission of Christian service. You don't have a job. You have a ministry. The Lord invites you to join Him in the Christian movement. It is a privilege to join God in what He is doing.

Most Christians understand that the preacher is "called" to ministry. Just about every Christian would say that pastors don't have a "job," but a calling from God. Believe it or not: Serving coffee and refreshments at your church is no different! Everything we do for God, big or small, wherever we do it, is a ministry. We represent the King of the universe!

We represent the King of the universe!

God never starts the process of ministry with a cry for help. Your baptism was your call into ministry. According to the New Testament, you become part of what is called the "royal priesthood." You are a minister, according to the New Testament. You serve with Jesus by divine design. Everything you do for Jesus is a ministry—at church or beyond. When you learn this, you might wonder, "How do Christians find their unique ministry—the calling that God has designed just for them?"

HOLY SPIRIT GIFTS

You have read references about spiritual gifts in previous chapters. In the context of church governance and ministry, we now look at this exciting dynamic in depth. When you receive the Holy Spirit, two miraculous events take place. First, you are given gifts. Second, these gifts direct you to your calling. Your calling guides you to your area of ministry. This is not like volunteerism, which *uses* you to get some job accomplished. Instead, God calls you to join Him in ministry through supernatural gifts given uniquely to you. Every Christian has a unique gift mix. Discovering these supernatural gifts is the first step toward finding the Lord's special calling for you. *Every* Christian is a minister. When you find your niche in ministry, you discover spiritual fulfillment.

The needs of the church do not define your ministry, nor do your personal ideas or wishes. God chooses your ministry. Your primary objective is to discover where God wants you. This raises the question, "How does God's system work?"

> ***Every* Christian is a minister.**

As a Christian, your first objective is to discover the gifts given uniquely to you by the Holy Spirit. Actually, you will discover what is called your *gift mix*. Every Christian has a divinely created mixture of gifts, whether they know about them or not. In the New Testament, there are three primary sections where spiritual gifts are listed. We looked briefly at this in a previous chapter. The primary locations in Scripture are Romans 12, 1 Corinthians 12, and Ephesians 4. Most biblical scholars will add a few other gifts that are scattered throughout the New Testament.

The way you discover your unique calling is to discern what gifts the Holy Spirit has given to you. The approach you will use to discover them begins by learning about them. Some Christians have studied spiritual gifts a lot. They have developed surveys to help you discover your own personal gift mix.[1]

GIFT DISCOVERY PROCESS

One of the best ways to learn about God's unique calling for you is to discover, develop, and use your spiritual gifts. This is the way the Holy Spirit guides you to your unique role of ministry in the body of Christ and beyond.

Becoming clear about your unique gift mix is a process. You experiment with the gifts. You observe whether or not the Lord affirms your ministry. Other Christians will affirm the results as well. Or, you may not receive that affirmation from others when you serve in certain areas. That does not make you a loser! There are no losers in the Kingdom of God. No one has all the gifts—except Jesus. Every believer has some spiritual gifts. As you experiment with your cluster of gifts, you will learn more about the unique gifts God has given you. In time, you will discover God's place for you in the body of Christ.

The next step is to hone your gifts. This is the *development stage*. For example, you may discover you have the gift of teaching. However, you may try teaching Sunday school or Vacation Bible School. As you do, you will learn more about whether teaching is one of your gifts. You may also learn that your teaching gift is strongest when you work with adults.

> **There are no losers in the Kingdom of God.**

As you learn about your gift mix, you will try several ministry opportunities. The more you are involved, the better, because you will begin to clarify which gifts in your cluster are more dominant and which ones are subordinate. Dominant gifts will show up stronger with a greater blessing of results. There will be evidence of positive results with your subordinate gifts as well. They just won't be as strong.

You will also explore your feelings. God has given you those feelings of satisfaction and fulfillment to help you discover His will and your place of ministry. As you use your gifts, God will direct you toward your calling—your place in the body of Christ. That calling is God's plan for your life and ministry. The next step is God's wonderful process of discipling.

DISCIPLING AND THE *APOSTOLIC COUNSEL*

There will be a variety of gifts that benefit the mission of your *apostolic counsel.* These have been mentioned in a previous chapter. If you are called to be on the counsel, some of your gifts will be used by God regularly. Other gifts in your mix may be used only occasionally.

As your church develops an *apostolic counsel,* it is important that you also use the discipleship process. The more you learn about discipling, the more you will realize how nominations and elections are foreign to God's approach! After a while, it will become clear: There is no better way to approach ministry other than God's way. You will also wonder how God's people could ever drift to the practices of nominations and elections for church governance or practice volunteerism for Christian service.

However, even though discovering spiritual gifts is the biblical approach to serving God, it isn't always perfect. Why? Not because God isn't perfect. It is because people are not perfect. So, beware: There may be some missteps in your journey. Just don't blame God or His process! And don't blame yourself or others. Thank God that He gives us the privilege to serve, in spite of our human challenges.

SIX STEPS OF THE DISCIPLESHIP PROCESS

Step #1: "Come follow me." You will likely recognize these words from Jesus. As you develop the mix of different gifts for your congregation's *apostolic counsel,* and as you identify those who reflect a strong lifestyle of biblical study, you will extend a *call* to those who you have identified as potential candidates for your church's decision-making ministry.

Thank God that He gives us the privilege to serve.

Who extends the call? It could be the (senior) pastor. Or, it could be the pastor, plus all or some of the existing leadership group of your church. This call is an *invitation* to start your congregation's *apostolic counsel.* Those invited represent, collectively, the gift mix you have predetermined is best for the counsel of your church.[2] This is the first step in the discipleship process. You are challenging these candidates to "come follow Jesus" into this counsel *and* to follow a discipleship process. This process includes on-the-job training, led by the pastor.

Step #2: "I do/you watch." At first, the pastor models the culture of an *apostolic counsel.* This process also includes teaching. Those chosen for the counsel will have already read about this form of governance. In this step, through the leadership of the pastor, those on the counsel are primarily focused on learning and growing into this biblical form of ministry.

Step #3: "I do/you help." In this stage, the value of the *apostolic counsel* model will already begin to show beneficial results. The process will be led by the pastor. Some members of the counsel will learn more quickly than others. They will begin to model the approach to others. Some of the early adopters model this approach to help others on the counsel.

Step #4: "You do/I help." At this level, the pastor gradually encourages more involvement by others on the *apostolic counsel.* They begin to feel more comfortable and contribute more often. At this point, it is important to remember the long-term value of this process.

Each member of the *apostolic counsel* will be asked to begin to pray for and look for—until they find—their own "disciple" to bring to the counsel. They will look for guidance and advice from the pastor and other members of the counsel. It is understood that they will develop this person through the discipleship model to become a future leader of the church. Remember, you are searching for someone who is known for biblical wisdom, based on a lifestyle of Bible study.

Do you see how seamless this style of leadership can be? You can begin to understand why it is far less disruptive than "nominations and elections—with term limits."

Step #5: "You do/I watch." While the pastor is never completely out of the leadership role, the involvement is less intense. As you consider Step 5, think about what happens in most churches if the pastor leaves, dies, or retires. When these major changes occur in many congregations, it is so disruptive! However, with discipled counsel members, the leadership is shared at a spiritual level, which makes major transitions much easier.

Step #6: "We all disciple the next generation of leaders for the *apostolic counsel*." This is when discipling becomes a lifestyle for leadership, just like it was for those in the New Testament. The apostles followed Jesus' model. Jesus did not recruit volunteers. He didn't nominate disciples. No one "voted." The disciples were chosen—invited—and discipled. Then, in the next generation, they discipled others.[3]

It is impossible to improve on the model that Jesus gave to the church. If you read the various letters in the New Testament, it is easy to see that the next generation of leaders is being discipled by the original leaders who served with Jesus.

Consider this: What if, at every level of the congregation's ministry, discipling became the dominant practice? What if everyone in the church discovered their spiritual gifts? What if Sunday school teachers, for example, followed the six steps of discipling with other potential Sunday school teachers, as they were "on the job" teaching Sunday school? What if this process was followed with worship leaders, ushers, Bible study teachers, outreach teams? Everyone? What if every ministry leader discipled a next generation leader, on the job, as they led their ministries? What if they used spiritual gifts as a defining factor in the process of inviting someone to be discipled into a unique ministry?

The process of discovering, developing, and using spiritual gifts is the "operating procedure and approach" for the Christian church. When the people of God grow spiritually, in a discipling culture, they have discovered—and operate from—their dominant and subordinate gifts. They have discovered *how* the Holy Spirit has uniquely chosen them for their calling to serve.

THE POWER OF MODELING

Jesus modeled how to lead in the Christian movement. His approach is not political, organizational, or dictatorial. His approach is *invitational*: "Come follow Me." It is developmental: "I will show you how to catch men and women." It is *motivational*: "As the Father sent Me, I send you." It is *inspirational*: "When the Holy Spirit comes, you will be able to be My witnesses." Jesus' approach is *practical*: "I chose you...to bear fruit that won't spoil." It is *powerful*: "...to the ends of the earth."

The movement launched by Jesus doesn't stop with the first disciples. They discipled others, who discipled others, who discipled more. This approach is designed as a spiritual movement for exponential multiplication.

> **Jesus modeled how to lead.**

If the pastor models discipling to those on the *apostolic counsel*, those on the counsel will catch what can't be taught: the *multiplication lifestyle* of discipling. If those on the *apostolic counsel* continue the multiplication lifestyle, they will model it to the rest of the congregation. Those in the church will *make* disciples who make disciples.

This culture of Kingdom dynamics simply can't be academically taught. It is more caught than taught. For example, beyond very rare exceptions, how do people become outstanding parents to their children? For most, it was modeled by *their* parents. That is why good parenting is generally multigenerational. In the body of Christ, if the leaders model multiplication by discipling, it will be caught by many in the church. In this way, the *apostolic counsel* model ignites a movement of multiplication. Leaders are the sparks that start the fire of revival. You simply cannot improve on Jesus' approach!

This culture of Kingdom dynamics is more caught than taught.

In the next chapter, we will focus on the practical dynamics for effectively changing over to an apostolic theocracy. You will operate by God's will, revealed in Scripture. You will lead others through relational influence: the apostolic model. In this next phase, we will outline the practical steps that have been effective for the transition to an *apostolic counsel.*

The *apostolic counsel* model ignites a movement of multiplication.

Reflective Questions for Chapter Seven: Jesus' Dynamic Approach

1. Have you been asked to "volunteer" at church? Has your involvement at church occasionally felt like a chore or duty? If so, did you feel a little guilty? Can you share your feelings with someone else—not to complain or criticize—but just to be honest?

2. Have you taken a survey to discover the spiritual gifts the Holy Spirit has given uniquely to you? Do you know what they are? If you don't, would you like to discover what supernatural gifts God has given you?

3. Have you attended a workshop or Bible class that explores the spiritual gifts listed in Romans 12, 1 Corinthians 12, Ephesians 4, and a few other New Testament verses? If you have, are you serving in the areas of your gift mix? Can you describe the difference it makes to be where God has *called you for ministry*? How is that different from the climate of volunteerism, in which the church is *using you to get a job done*?

4. Have you been discipled to serve in your unique niche, based on the spiritual gifts God has given you? Have you been involved in the six steps of the discipleship process? Have you discipled others following those six steps? If you have children, have you discipled them using the six steps demonstrated by Jesus and the apostles? How often is this process used to develop service opportunities for those in your church?

CHAPTER EIGHT

Transforming Your Church to an Apostolic Theocracy

Church leaders meet with agendas. Spiritual leaders meet with Bibles.

"Counsel and sound judgment are mine; I have insight, I have power."

— Proverbs 8:14 (New International Version)

In the last chapter, we looked at two primary practices unique to the New Testament operational approach. The first is the focus on discovering, developing, and using your spiritual gifts. Spiritual gifts represent the discerning process that leads Christ-followers to discover God's calling on their lives. Your spiritual gifts direct you to your chosen area of ministry. When you find your calling, you experience your greatest impact for God. As He uses you in your divine "sweet spot," you discover meaningful fulfillment.

The second operational approach is the process of discipling, as modeled by Jesus, His disciples, and millions of believers throughout history—whenever Christianity has flourished. Discipleship includes teaching and learning. Most of all, it includes on-the-job training—what some call apprenticing. The six steps of discipling are fundamental to the effectiveness of the Christian movement. The practice of volunteerism is foreign to Jesus' approach.

In this chapter, we explore the implementation phase of transforming a local church to an apostolic theocracy model of church governance. A *theocracy* is the cultural statement of priority: "We want what God wants." It reflects what believers pray in the Lord's Prayer: "...your will be done, on earth as it is in heaven."[1] What God wants is found in the Bible. The Scripture has no reference to a constitution, nominations, elections, majority rule, or Robert's Rules of Order.

Instead, God provides counsel. In Scripture, God is called "Counselor."[2] Jesus discipled followers by teaching them the counsel of God, which He has given to us in Scripture. There is no evidence of politics or votes or majority rule to discern what God wants His people to do. In fact, to even think so might be considered a practice of idolatry!

The leaders who followed Jesus were called "disciples," and after the resurrection, "apostles." They developed no laws or bylaws for the church, which Jesus proclaimed *He* would build.[3] The apostles actually avoided political pressure or legalistic approaches to influence the Christians they led.

The *apostolic* approach is characterized by two primary elements: (1) the teaching of Scripture and (2) relational capital. God's people followed what the apostles wrote in letters or taught in person. Healthy congregations in the Jesus movement continue to follow what is written. The "leverage" used by the writers of the New Testament letters is the same as that of Jesus. People

> **The *apostolic* approach is characterized by the teaching of Scripture and relational capital.**

wanted to do what Jesus said because of (1) His *divine relationship* with the Father (2) and His *spiritual relationship* with His followers. *Jesus rules by love, not by regulations or votes*. His death on the cross was not a political statement. It was a sacrifice of relational love. These are the two elements of an *apostolic counsel* that Jesus will use to lead your church: (1) God's will and (2) relational influence.

PARADIGM SHIFT

Over time, God's people often drift toward political control—even though, for those who know Scripture, it doesn't "feel" right. Many Christians "inherit" legalistic decision-making imprinted by worldly nuance. It is a major paradigm shift for God's people to move from bylaws to biblical decision-making.

Why? Part of the reason is that legalism is easier. You don't have to think. You don't have to pray. Legalism doesn't require knowing the Scripture in order to discern God's will. Honestly, the biblical approach is more work.

However, God's way is so much better! God's will is always right. God's approach works best. Changing a congregation's governance is an act like repentance: changing direction. It is not easy, because it is a major paradigm shift. Yet, it is always best. If this sounds challenging, it is because it is transformational. Think about it: The apostle writes, "Do not be conformed to this world but be transformed by the renewal of your mind...."[4] It is a change in the way you think.

> **Legalism is easier. You don't have to think.**

THE VALUE OF INTERVENTION

As we have worked with hundreds of congregations, it has been clear: A little help from those outside can be of great value. It is why God sent prophets. It is why Jesus came to earth. It is why the apostles visited the young churches. It is also why smart people see their physicians.

Physicians practice *diagnosis*—discovering the symptoms; *prognosis*—providing alternative outcomes, with or without help; and *prescriptions*—a proposed direction toward a favorable outcome. This approach is greatly helpful for the human body. It is also beneficial for the body of Christ. The Head of the church is perfect. From the neck on down, the church consists of real people, with all our frailties. Seasoned expert guidance based on biblical truth provides great help. This is what the letters of the New Testament are all about.

DIAGNOSTIC SURVEY

To start the process of moving toward an *apostolic counsel*, we at Church Doctor developed a diagnostic survey focused on church governance. It is called the Church Government Consultation Survey. It was developed in our ministry "lab," field-tested, and improved over a period of thirteen years. It represents the *diagnosis* phase of the diagnosis-prognosis-prescription, mentioned above.

This survey helps church leaders think about the hundreds of parts and pieces of decision-making in every congregation. (If governance was simple, Christians would have figured it out by themselves a long time ago.) The survey provides multiple-choice responses to the numerous nuances of church decision-making. The choices include popular approaches, along with a biblical choice for each element in the decision-making process. Scripture *does* speak to all aspects of the decision-making process. Unfortunately, they are scattered all over the Bible. They are embedded in the survey, among the questions and multiple-choice answers.

The survey is given to (1) everyone on staff, (2) anyone who is a "leader," in any area of the church ministry. The results are scored by a Church Doctor analyst, comparing staff and leadership in the process. Later in the process, the survey is offered to any member of the congregation who would like to participate. For those who are interested, the survey stimulates the thinking process of how a church makes decisions. For many, it provides an "aha" moment.

ISSUE BEHIND THE ISSUES

One of the foundational elements of an effective decision-making environment is the nature, function, and purpose of a church. Clarity about these basics greatly impacts the effectiveness of every congregation, every local gathering of Christians, or groups of churches—often called denominations, fellowships, dioceses, or synods.

The Church Government Consultation Survey guides church leaders and staff to focus on the *nature of the church*. The church of New Testament Christianity is unique. Most Christians understand that the church is not like any other organization. So, how is it that decision-making approaches drift so far from what God intends? The survey process helps Christians to think at deeper levels about their congregation. Technically, this is called *ecclesiology*—the study of the nature, function, and purpose of the church.

In the following pages, we look at the biblical uniqueness of the church at a deeper level. The Church Government Consultation Survey is used to diagnose areas of strength and weakness in a church. The nature, function, and purpose of the biblical church is quite complex. Yet, it serves as the driving force that shapes church governance. The following diagram represents the unique DNA of the church. For each biblical component, there is an *opposite* structural approach.

These variables shape the decision-making approach we call church governance. Some are polar opposites. Clarity about each of them is essential for developing an apostolic theocracy. Look at the following diagram as a wheel.

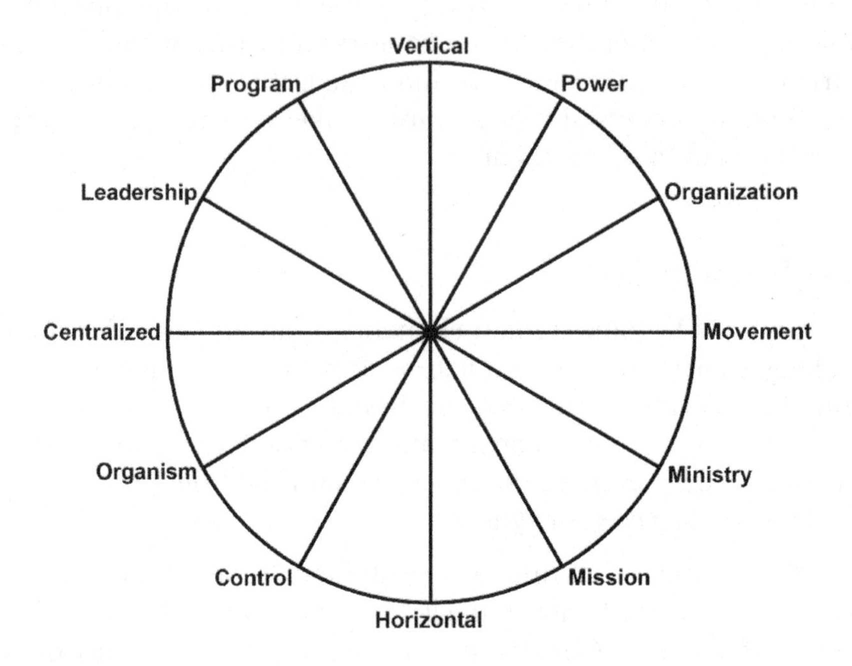

There is no top or bottom. Instead, these are characteristics of biblical church and opposite characteristics. There is some overlap in emphasis. As you study this graphic and read about it, consider which areas should be more dominant or less dominant in the decision-making process.

VERTICAL-HORIZONTAL

Jesus came to this earth, often referred to as "down from heaven." After the resurrection, He "ascended" into heaven. So, should a church or denomination be ruled vertically by a top-down mechanism? Not really. Why? Because Jesus launched a horizontal approach to build His Kingdom. He modeled it with His disciples. The apostles modeled it in the New Testament churches. Church people shared the Good News about Jesus with others: person to person—horizontally.

Jesus launched a horizontal approach.

CENTRALIZED-MOVEMENT

The New Testament references "the church at Jerusalem." It also speaks about the church at Rome, one at Galatia, the church at Ephesus, and others. In truth, these were not megachurches—stand-alone congregational centers for each city. Most of them were scattered house churches.

Christians, by design, are called to share the Good News of Jesus, movement-style. This fits with the multiplication model God clearly demonstrates. He said to Adam and Eve, "Be fruitful and multiply." Jesus, in the Great Commission, says, "Go make disciples." This is essentially the same idea. Churches birth churches, and Christians reach others. All of what God does is movement-oriented.

> **All of what God does is movement-oriented.**

ORGANIZATION-ORGANISM

Most Christians subconsciously drift toward the concept of the church as organization. Many churches perpetuate that concept by their approach to decision-making—their church governance. To be clear, for a movement to become effective, it needs to be somewhat organized. It is beneficial to have plans, goals, and objectives.

However, the "church" is described in the New Testament using a variety of metaphors: the sheep and the Shepherd, the family of God, the household of God, the Vine and the branches, the priesthood of believers—and more. Every one of these descriptions reflects a living organism. Your human body is wonderfully *organized*. Yet, it is a living *organism*, not an organization.

The church is dynamic, living, growing. It is more than an organization that *produces* something. It is a body of believers.

Each one is to *reproduce* others who are rebirthed—born again. There is no "business as usual" in the design of the church, no bureaucracy of organization intended. Your church is functional, alive, growing, multiplying—or should be!

PROGRAM-MISSION

Every church has programs. These are internal spiritual activities, like worship, Sunday school, Bible classes, etc. They are programmatic. They are programmed. They are the internal functions of a church. Yet, they are not or should not be similar to other organizations. Everything a church might do should go beyond maintenance. It is valuable to maintain spiritual health, yet every activity—even "programs"—should have *external* goals. Jesus was on a mission. His disciples were on a mission. Christians are to be "on mission" 24/7. A church that is preoccupied with maintenance—even "theological" maintenance—has lost its vitality. Mission is the lifeblood of the vibrant church. Good theology is nonnegotiable. Pure doctrine, in the absence of mission, is the body of Christ on life support.

POWER-CONTROL

It is human nature to default toward control. It is a temptation for every Christian, denomination, and church to subconsciously try to control. In contrast, when a "revival" breaks out, the movement of those becoming Christians is, literally, out of (human) control. If your primary focus is on control, you will never experience movement. Think of the Roman Catholic Church at the time of the Reformation. The Church was steeped in rules, regulations, orders, and bishops. Worship was in Latin, which few people understood. It was what missiologists call a *closed set*. You are

> **Pure doctrine, in absence of mission, is the Body of Christ on life support.**

either all in or out. When Luther and other reformers were declared "out," they were liberated to form churches that spoke to the masses on the basics of "Scripture alone, faith alone, and grace alone." Once the control was no longer effective, the movement flourished. A movement flourishes beyond the restrictions of control. The New Testament Church was birthed within the tensions created by the scribes and Pharisees, who lost control—and lost many of their followers.

There are two related issues: faith and religion. Faith is trust in God to give up human control. It is faith in the Scripture to guide and control the destiny of the Christian movement, down to the smallest detail. Human nature drifts toward religion: the way we do this and that, the programmatic approach, the styles, the dress codes, the pews, the buildings, the rituals, and the way we've always done it.

Religion loves rules and regularities. Why? They bring the "comfort" of human control. It becomes a faith in religion rather than belief in God. He is always changing styles and approaches: whatever it takes to deliver the unchanging essence of Christian faith to a constantly changing world.

Faith is trust in God to give up human control.

The question should be: Where is the power? If the power is centralized, the movement is doomed. Why? It is not faith in God. It becomes faith in ourselves, our rules, our traditions, our politics, and our votes. Most of the Pharisees were stuck in the rut of power. Jesus, on the other hand, gave the Holy Spirit to every believer. He put the power in the heart and hands of every Christ-follower. The Scripture says, "...to all who received him, who believed in his name, he gave power to become children of God...."[5] He was not speaking to a board. He was promising the Spirit and His supernatural gifts to everyone who is a child of God. This leads to the last distinction about God's gifts of leadership and ministry.

MINISTRY-LEADERSHIP

Some Christians relegate "ministry" to leaders and staff and allow the masses to be "volunteers," as was mentioned in a previous chapter. Yet, Jesus spent most of His time developing twelve ordinary guys for ministry. He never said, "Can I get a volunteer?" The disciples became disciplers who discipled other disciples—and so the movement began. This approach is not just about growth: It is explosive! The New Testament calls this the "royal priesthood" or "priesthood of all believers."[6] It is abundantly clear: Every Christian is a minister. Every Christian has a ministry. Your baptism is your ordination to ministry. It is repeated here as a distinction between ministry and leadership.

This is the power of movement multiplication. The Scripture says there are leader-type gifts/roles: apostles, prophets, evangelists, pastors, and teachers. Their expressed calling is *not* to do ministry for Christians. It is "to equip Christians to do the work of ministry." Church staff should almost never do ministry alone. From the movement perspective, they should follow the model of Jesus: "Follow me."[7] This is a powerful movement dynamic. Every Christian has been given a spiritual DNA gift mix by the Holy Spirit. When you discover and develop your gifts, you find your God-designed ministry. No one has a job at church. You have a calling to reach the world, hand in hand with the Ruler of the universe. You have supernatural gifts to use for your mission.

As you develop an *apostolic counsel* for your church, you will develop a list of dominant and subordinate gifts that will serve your church best at this time in history. Spiritual gifts and a lifestyle of Bible study are the two most important components for identifying those who will serve on the counsel.

You have a calling to reach the world.

It was my mentor, Dr. C. Peter Wagner, who taught me the key balance of effort between leadership and ministry in ratio to the pastor/staff and the congregational members.[8]

THE ROLE OF LEADERSHIP

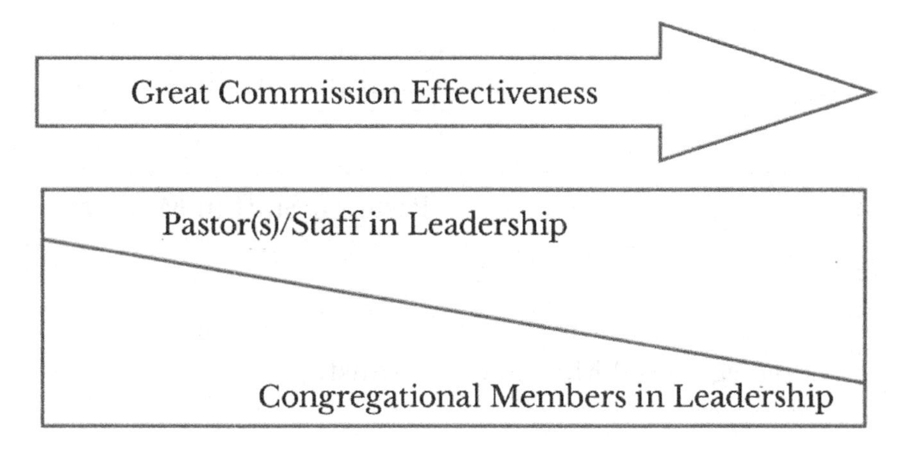

The graphic above shows what research has demonstrated in churches about *leadership*: The more pastor(s) and staff operate as *leaders* (decision-makers, equippers) and, by contrast, the less that congregational members try to lead the church (make decisions), the greater the effectiveness (end result) of the Great Commission objectives: make disciples, grow the church, reach people for Christ, and impact the community, the nation, and the world.

Notice: The graphic indicates that pastors and staff do not entirely lead, nor are congregational members entirely out of leadership. (This is why the graphic dividing line is not placed in the exact corners.) Observation and research show that Great Commission effectiveness occurs when leadership generally leads and a smaller portion of the congregation is included in leadership. Ideally, those with the gift of leadership will lead an area of ministry into which they have been discipled. Of course, those on the *apostolic counsel* would be part of the leadership.

THE ROLE OF MINISTRY

Great Commission Effectiveness

Pastor(s)/Staff in Ministry

Congregational Members in Ministry

The graphic above shows what research has demonstrated in churches about *ministry*: The more congregational members operate in *ministry* (service, hospital calling, outreach, Christian counseling, witnessing, etc.) the greater the effectiveness. By contrast, the less the pastor(s) and staff are involved in ministry, the greater effectiveness. The end result is an increase in the Great Commission objectives: make disciples, grow the church, reach people for Christ, and impact the community, the nation, and the world. This approach implies that members, once discipled, disciple others. It reflects the New Testament model of explosive multiplication. It reflects a movement, not an organization.

Notice: The graphic indicates that congregational members do not *entirely* do ministry, nor are leaders (pastors and staff) *entirely* out of ministry. (This is why the graphic dividing line is not placed in the exact corners.) Observation and research show that Great Commission effectiveness occurs when congregational members generally do ministry with a smaller effort by pastor(s) and staff doing ministry. Ideally, staff never do ministry alone, but equip and disciple church members as they serve.

In the next chapter we will look at more key elements that help your church develop an *apostolic counsel.*

Reflective Questions for Chapter Eight: Transforming Your Church to an Apostolic Theocracy

1. As the title of this chapter implies, the apostolic theocracy approach demonstrated in the Bible *transforms* your church. It is a different way of thinking. In Romans 12:2, the Apostle Paul writes, "Do not be conformed to this world...." Have you ever thought about how church governance—decision-making in the church—conforms to human politics? Paul continues: "...but be transformed by the renewal of your mind...." Do you *think* a biblical approach to decision-making would transform your church? How would it impact whole denominations?

2. How would you describe the *nature* of the church? How is the "church" unique? What characteristics are special about the church? What do you think is the main *function* of a church? Is it simply to serve the desires and needs of the members? What is the *purpose* of the church? Is it limited to maintaining, or does it include reaching the world? How do these issues relate to the way church leaders make decisions about your church?

3. As you review the graphic that looks like the spokes of a wheel, notice that each "spoke" of the wheel has two ends, representing opposite dynamics. These complex issues require some thought and processing. Think about how you look at your church. How do you understand these dynamics? How does your church reflect each one? What requires change? What should stay the same?

4. Study the graphics about Great Commission effectiveness and the two basic roles: leadership and ministry. What does this say to you about the role of *leadership*? What does it tell you about the role of *ministry*? How do these concepts fit your church? What should change?

CHAPTER NINE

Functions of Decision-Making

Many church people play politics. Spiritual leaders seek God's will.

"The Spirit of the Lord will rest on him—the Spirit of wisdom and of understanding, the Spirit of counsel and of might, the Spirit of the knowledge and fear of the Lord...."

— Isaiah 11:2 (New International Version)

In the last chapter, we began to look at the implementation phase for moving your congregation toward a biblical form of church governance. We focused on the nature, function, and purpose of the church according to the Scripture. We looked at a few of the key issues that are identified through the Church Government Consultation Survey.

The study of the biblical nature of the church is called ecclesiology. It has several dimensions: vertical and horizontal; centralized and movement; organization and organism; program and mission; power and control; ministry and leadership.

In this chapter, we explore other elements included in the Church Government Consultation Survey. These areas are important as you develop a biblical form of decision-making. You will likely realize that church governance has many nuances. Almost always, these issues are *assumed*: "Everyone knows that," so we think! *The purpose of this chapter is to examine some of the nuts-and-bolts issues of how to direct your church.* The survey is constructed to provide input from leaders and staff—*and* congregational members. In every church, the results are enlightening! In Chapter Ten, we will focus on the "nuts and bolts" of how we help leaders transition to a form of church governance that greatly improves their decision-making and is personalized to the uniqueness of their congregation or denomination.

PURPOSE AND PRIORITIES OF THE LOCAL CHURCH

In the Church Government Consultation Survey Church Doctor Ministries developed for congregations, we focus on four common approaches that clarify the basic purpose and priorities of your church. From a biblical perspective, as well as practical effectiveness, congregations generally fall into one of four categories of decision-making: (1) majority rule; (2) the reasoning of a decision-making group; (3) the insight and vision of the senior leader and a group organized to protect the church from a "dictator"; or (4) the direction of Christ, discovered through Scripture, an *apostolic counsel*. Most congregations dabble in the use of several of these areas in one aspect or another.

For those who confess that Scripture is God's Word, it seems like a no-brainer! However, history has already demonstrated that God's people are subject to biblical drift. The Protestant Reformation was, to a large degree, fueled by this reality. (At this point in history, perhaps the Christian movement is in need of another season of reform.) By asking survey questions, Christians don't simply consider the issues academically. The survey launches a wake-up call to everyone in the church.

This is a good place to reflect on why the survey questions work well to energize Christ-followers to focus at a deeper level. When guiding people of faith to make change, dictatorial approaches are not always the most effective. You've probably heard, and perhaps used the words, "I feel you are preaching at me!"

The cue for effective improvement in the life of the church comes from Jesus Himself. The Savior is the most brilliant leader in history. If you need proof, you only need to look at the number of followers, the longevity of the movement, and the multicultural forms of expression of the same basic truths. There is no movement in history, measured by any scale, that comes close.

This amazing leader, Jesus, is a master at influencing others. One of His many tactics was exercised when He dealt with challenging issues. Yes, He did a lot of preaching. He also nuanced His influence, when appropriate, by teaching. He cemented a new, comprehensive lifestyle approach by discipling. *However, when issues were super complex, He asked questions.* This approach, in modern history, is called "interrogative influence." One example stands out. Remember when Jesus asked the disciples, "Who do people say the Son of Man is?" Then He drilled deeper: "But what about you?" He asked. "Who do *you* say I am?"[1] He could have just said, "Look, I'm getting crucified soon and, later, ascending into heaven. I need to make sure you're ready to carry on. You know I'm the Lord, the Son of the living God. Don't forget it." It is likely that approach would have been way too strong. It could be called an "emotional dump." Sadly, it is used often in church politics!

Interrogative influence is the power of asking questions. It makes others think deeply. They don't feel like they are being "pushed." This is why using survey questions is powerful! How the body of Christ—your church—makes decisions is an emotional area. Honestly? Most Christians have inherited forms of decision-making that actually hurt more than help. They divide more than unite. The better you understand this, the more you will wonder about most church decision-making practices.

THE DECISION-MAKING ROLE

In the survey we developed for church governance, we ask about the primary role of a church decision-making group. Actually, those who guide a church through decisions have several roles. Yet, there is—or should be—clarity about their *primary function*. Without clarity, decision-makers lose critical focus. Sadly, this occurs frequently in local churches and even more so in denominational entities at regional and national levels.

The choices for role definition of decision-making groups usually fall into four categories. When drift occurs, due to lack of clarity, they can wander all over the decision-making landscape.

CATEGORY #1: PURE DEMOCRACY

Ask yourself: Should the decision-makers represent the *majority* thinking of all the members of your local church? This approach is called "pure democracy." Consider this in the Bruce family of four: mom, dad, fifteen-year-old Kailyn, and five-year-old Julianna. A decision must be made: "Pay the mortgage, or go to Disney World?" The vote respects everyone equally. It is also an insane way to run a family—including the church family.

While this pure democracy borders on the absurd, in many churches, this is exactly what occurs. It is defined as a *congregational* form of governance. So, if a new Christian, like Julianna, goes through a "membership class" and gets baptized, her input is equal to seventy-year-old David and Audrey, who have been in a weekly Bible class for fifty years. It really gets tricky when fifty-five-year-old Mike becomes a Christian and instantly has equal decision-making input, but can't find Ephesians in the Bible. Is that a biblical approach? Yet, many congregations and denominational meetings operate precisely this way!

CATEGORY #2: A REPUBLIC FORM OF GOVERNMENT

A second choice for the decision-making group allows for input from the masses because "they support the church financially, and their wishes should be carried out." In this approach, those who are "nominated" and "elected" by the members become the decision-making group. They make decisions that represent—in theory—the wishes of all the members.

This is called a "republic" form of governance. In most churches, those who are nominated for a leadership decision-making role are rarely vetted based on Scripture knowledge, awareness of spiritual gifts, or clarity about the primary mission of the church. Most often, someone randomly picked to be on a "nominating committee" calls a person to ask if they "would be willing to run" for a position or office. This was covered in an earlier chapter, but it is worth expanding further because it sets the tone for the popular republic form of governance used in many churches.

This approach is fascinating on three levels in the culture of a Christian church. First, most positions for nominations require at least two people to "run" for one position. Keep asking these reasonable—and biblical—questions: *"Why should anyone willing to serve God and the church lose an election in front of all their fellow Christian friends?" How does that sync with the tone of Scripture and the will of God?*

On a second level, the republic form of governance has a false understanding about service. There are no "jobs" in the church of Jesus Christ. Many churches focus on "volunteerism" as if it was "baptized" by Jesus Himself. (You've already read a lot about that! Now do you see how this relates to the election process?) You won't find a verse in the four Gospels of the New Testament where Jesus says, "Can I get a volunteer?" In truth, the concept of a "volunteer" is nowhere to be found in Scripture. Service in the Kingdom is a sacred gift and opportunity. It is a "ministry." God doesn't *use* people—as though He is desperate to complete a job that He can't do by Himself. Instead, God wants to give His followers the privilege of sharing in His eternal, divine work.

In the makeup of the organism called "church," every person has a high calling. (This was also covered in an earlier chapter.) Everyone is a minister. Some translations of Scripture call it the "royal priesthood"—you are a minister for the King of the universe. You identify your calling by discovering your spiritual gifts. Yet, in the republic form of governance, the church *uses people who are most willing to be nominated, but often have no clue about their spiritual gifts.* Therefore, they can't know if God has called them to serve in that area.

On the third level of the "republic" approach to governance, most of those who are nominated to "run" for a position are highly visible members of the local community. They may include successful business owners, doctors, lawyers, teachers, and others who are well-known in the public sector.

Churches and denominations almost always have a constitutional paragraph that states that their basic source for operation is Scripture. Yet, the visible, high-profile community leaders may—*or may not*—be conversant with the depths of Scripture. However, as "community leaders," they may have the "confidence"—more than others—to stand at a church meeting and voice their opinions. Consequently, they are more likely to be nominated and elected to governance positions. Their biblical knowledge, especially in the area of ecclesiology (the nature, purpose, and function of the church) may be extremely limited! Almost every pastor could name a person, well-known in the community, who gets into a position in the church and, out of biblical ignorance, influences the church toward bad decisions. It is one of the most common reasons pastors lose sleep.

CATEGORY #3: CHECKS AND BALANCES PROTECTION

As a variation of the republic form of church governance, some churches develop a group of leaders whose job it is to "police the pastor and staff" (though it is never described that way). They are a group of church leaders who function as a "balance of power," so the pastor and staff do not drift into a "dictatorship" model. They may—or may not—serve from a perspective of biblical depth.

Often this group is elected. However, in some churches, they are chosen by the pastor. They are often called "elders" or "deacons." In other congregations, they are the "consistory" or "session." Often, they have a vote, equal to—or collectively greater than—the pastor and the staff.

It is common for high-profile civic and business leaders to subconsciously default toward worldly business approaches for the "Lord's work." Unless they are equipped uniquely in the "mind of Christ," they will subconsciously direct the church down a secular path. It is possible to be an intelligent person, yet ignorant of biblical uniqueness. Jesus was very clear: "My kingdom is not of (not like) this world."[2] Without depth in Scripture, great leaders—who mean well—corrupt the church decision-making process by including checks and balances in church governance.

CATEGORY #4: APOSTOLIC COUNSEL

So, what is the *best* governance approach and primary role of the church decision-making group? The biblical approach is focused on the concept of *ministry*. It is not just ministry to or through the church. It is ministry to the pastor(s) and staff. The *apostolic counsel* is focused on support. This includes guidance for those who are part-time or full-time workers who live church 24/7. Their greatest need is biblically based spiritual support. In an *apostolic counsel* approach, the focus is not on leadership, but ministry: to the pastor(s), to the staff, to the church.

Scripture does identify those who are in key leadership "positions" of the church, as previously mentioned. In Ephesians 4, Paul lists them as apostles, prophets, evangelists, pastors, and teachers. These are the "callings" in the body of Christ. These believers have a special role. It is not simply to "do" ministry on behalf of the rest. Apostles, prophets, evangelists, pastors, and teachers are "to equip the saints for the work of ministry...."[3] (Notice it does not say "for the work of leadership.")

In an *apostolic counsel* approach, the focus is not on leadership, but ministry.

From the biblical approach, the leadership positions—apostles, prophets, evangelists, pastors, and teachers—are not geared toward political power. These roles are equipping roles. However, they are not "hired hands" to do the ministry. Their primary role is to *equip* Christians for ministry.

Consider this biblical approach compared to most churches. In many congregations, if a person is sick and in the hospital, they *expect* the pastor to visit them. However, the biblical approach makes it clear: Multiplication of ministry is a priority. The pastor should always take someone along who has the gift mix for hospital ministry. They should be discipled into that ministry—equipped for that calling. As they serve in that capacity and become proficient, they will do it on their own. Yet, they, too, will never do it alone. They also will multiply by discipling others who have spiritual gifts in that area—a "calling" to serve in that way. Ultimately, this model frees staff from ministry roles.

Apostles, prophets, evangelists, pastors and teachers are equipping roles.

The biblical approach focuses on *mission*. Politically oriented approaches bog down leaders in decision-making minutiae. The focus is on "running the church machine" smoothly. This approach limits key leaders and staff to a maintenance paradigm. The mission vision is crippled. The church subtly moves into maintenance mode. The outreach and growth stalls. The median age of members gets older. The church declines.

So, what, then, is the role of staff leaders? It is to multiply churches! Churches plant new churches. Staff leaders who equip members to do ministry have the time and energy to multiply the church. This exponential reality is basic to the Christian movement! Paul, Peter, and Luke did not simply start a church. They empowered their churches to start other churches.

Jesus modeled this approach. So did the apostles. This approach changes the church from "program" orientation to "mission and ministry." If you want to know how far most churches have drifted, consider the pastor who disciples a member to minister to those who need Christian counseling. The member who counsels is discipling another member in that ministry. The person seeking counseling comes in, and the first thing she says is, "Where is the pastor?" And she thinks, "What do we pay the pastor for, anyway?" The potential for revival is truncated by that mindset!

In the biblical approach to church—the New Testament culture—the primary role of the decision-making group is "to support, encourage, and guide the pastor(s) and staff." The pastor(s) and staff disciple and engage the people in ministry. As the movement matures, the pastors and staff multiply churches. As they do, they disciple members of the church with the right gift mix to lead those churches. All heaven rejoices. Control politicians freak out. Yet, God's Kingdom grows! That is the *movement* called Christianity. The governance survey gently guides Christians in a path that leads to mission effectiveness.

When looking at these four approaches to governance, there is a surprising result. Most leaders and church members actually choose the correct biblical answer—what we call an *apostolic counsel.* When they see the results of the survey, they realize the vast majority of people agree: The governance model should be one that supports the pastor and the staff. If they follow through, their church begins a journey with great potential!

When the survey results are made public, the common response is, "Why do we do church the way we do? How did we get so messed up?" This signals that most Christians are more ready to make positive change in the area of church governance than others would ever guess! Church governance is not the only element that ignites the church for revival. However, it greatly reduces the roadblocks and allows the church to blossom toward more effective Great Commission ministry.[4]

In the next chapter, we will focus on how your church can implement a new form of church governance. This is a critical and challenging phase for most church leaders. As you will discover, the transition to a biblical approach to church governance does not work best as an abrupt either/or "event." It succeeds through a both/and "process."

Reflective Questions for Chapter Nine: Functions of Decision-Making

1. This chapter reflects key issues that impact decision-making. Four approaches to decision-making in churches include: (1) majority rule; (2) the reasoning of a decision-making group; (3) the insight and vision of a leader; and (4) the direction of Christ discovered through Scripture—the role of an *apostolic counsel*. Which model best represents the decision-making process at your church? What are the benefits of that model? What are the challenges or weaknesses?

2. One of the leadership teaching approaches often used by Jesus can be described as *interrogative influence*. Jesus helped people learn by asking questions. Effective leadership isn't about "pushing" people, but about coaching them to new and better insights. Are you a parent? If not, you had parents or others who stood in that role for you. How does this approach work, in your experience? How often is this leadership style practiced in your church?

3. Look at the four general approaches churches use to make decisions: (1) pure democracy; (2) republic; (3) checks and balances protection; and (4) *apostolic counsel*. Which one best resembles the approach of your church? Which one best resembles how you make decisions? Which approach would work best in your church? If your church is part of a denomination or network of congregations, how would it work at that level?

4. To what degree does your church rely on the pastor and paid staff? Do they focus on performing ministry or on equipping church members to do ministry? Is the staff multiplying ministry among others? Are you? If you have children, are you helping them to discover their spiritual gifts? Are you discipling them to use their gifts to serve God's Kingdom? Are you discipling anyone? From the Kingdom perspective, how are you multiplying yourself?

CHAPTER TEN

Launching a Biblical Approach

Many Christians vote the majority; biblical leaders pray for consensus.

"The counsel of the Lord stands for ever, the thoughts of his heart to all generations."

—Psalm 33:11 (Revised Standard Version)

In the last chapter, we focused on some of the basic issues we use to approach church governance. Most congregations and denominations, as well as parachurch organizations, use a form of decision-making that is one, or a combination of, the following: (1) pure democracy, (2) republic, (3) checks and balances for staff, (4) apostolic theocracy.

In this chapter, we look at the transition process and some of the nuts-and-bolts practical issues involved in changing to a biblical form of church governance. Since it is a major paradigm shift, you will likely benefit from the use of a guide, coach, or consultant who has been "down this road" and who can answer questions and cast vision for this much better way to "do church."

An apostolic theocracy, nonpolitical approach works best because it is biblical. While "councils" in the New Testament are political, "counsels"—also in the New Testament—are based on seeking God's will from Scripture. A "theocracy" simply means "we want what God wants; our focus is on God's direction found in Scripture." The apostolic approach is clear and consistent in the New Testament. There are no politics or votes. Prayer and Christian principles are used to reach consensus.

The *apostolic counsel* form of church governance is focused on supporting and encouraging a small group of "called" believers. They follow biblical direction and prayerfully seek God's will. This approach presumes that those who are chosen—not elected—for an *apostolic counsel* are known for their lifestyle as serious students of Scripture. When challenging decisions are necessary, they search Scripture, discuss, and pray, rather than vote. They seek unanimous consensus. If they do not reach consensus, they "wait on the Lord"—and do not make a decision until there is consensus.

While some may feel this approach is "too idealistic, it will never work," in truth, those Christians and their churches, guided and directed through the process, have all discovered that it does work. They have continued to follow it and discovered a peaceful and joyful approach to making decisions. Some of the early churches that participated have used this biblical approach to church governance for more than twenty years. Those involved include congregations of all sizes from many different ecclesiastical backgrounds. This approach has also been used in several parachurch organizations and in at least one denomination with churches in both the United States and Canada. The reaction to this biblical form of church governance has consistently resulted in two responses: "We are liberated by the refreshing joy of making decisions this way," and "Why did we ever get involved in the way we used to do it?"

Changing church governance is a major paradigm shift for most Christians. It is similar to the flat earth theory. For centuries, most everyone was convinced that the earth was flat. They explained that "the rising of the morning sun" revealed that the sun revolved around the earth. Nevertheless, it was always true that the earth was round and revolved around the sun. It was a major paradigm shift when people sailed across the ocean and did not fall off the earth! This became an epochal change. It came with numerous consequences! A careful and thorough study of the New Testament provides a dramatic paradigm shift about how to operate the local church, denominations, and parachurch organizations.[1]

Changing church governance is a major paradigm shift.

THE WAY TO START

If you have read this book, you have already started the launch phase to consider a new, biblical form of decision-making. In the early part of this book, we looked at the different choices for church governance that have been used in history. Now, you want to share it with others who have influence in your church. Remember, most Christians accept several erroneous conclusions about church governance: (1) the way we make decisions is 100 percent biblical; (2) every church, denomination, and Christian parachurch ministry must make decisions the same way; (3) this is the way we've always done it; (4) there are no other options; and (5) the way we do it must be the best, most efficient way to do God's work.

While none of these assumptions are accurate, you can't "force-feed" change. Whatever form of church governance you have used, it feels "normal" to most of those in your church. Remember, if Christians believe the approach you use to make decisions is "sacred" and "important," the transition will include a biblical paradigm shift.

In almost every church, there are a few whose favorite "Bible verse" is: "But we have always done it this way!" This concept actually appears in the New Testament. It was the frequent objection of the Pharisees. Remember, Saul was the persecutor of Christ-followers in the early days of the Jesus movement. That side of Saul represents the "patron saint" of many "church bullies." Scripture says: "The good acquire a taste for helpful conversations; bullies push and shove their way through life (Proverbs 13:2, *The Message*). Most churches have one or two of them. They are vocal about change, and they take refuge in political structures. Why? They want to leverage their influence. Pray for them to have their own "Damascus road experience." Focus on Scripture. Love them like Jesus would. Pray for transformation.

It is helpful to unpack the various forms of church governance. Help those in your church discover the *reason* for decision-making. For many, the primary criterion is: "It works"—though not very well! Others will add that the priority for decision-making is to operate "decently and in order." That is not a bad idea, but it is far short of a biblical approach to church life, according to God's will.

Your fellow Christians will need to be led in thinking about (1) how Christ-followers uniquely make decisions; (2) what is the nature, purpose, and function of the church, according to Scripture; (3) how the apostles operated in the New Testament church; (4) why the early Christian movement turned away from politically packed councils to counsel-based decision-making; and (5) the major impact the biblical decision-making process has on the primary mission effectiveness of your church.

> **Help those in your church discover the *reason* for decision-making.**

In that discussion, another major, biblical paradigm shift will take place. *Volunteerism*, no matter how sacred religious people try to make it, is not a biblical approach to serve in the church. Six biblical teachings will be resurrected in the process of changing to a biblical approach of decision-making: (1) everyone is a minister in the royal priesthood of believers; (2) every Christian has a ministry; (3) your ministry is a personal *calling* given to you by God—not a job "to help the church"; (4) you will find your calling when you discover, develop, and use your unique spiritual gifts, given by the Holy Spirit; (5) as you find your calling in and through the body of Christ, you experience divine fulfillment; and (6) as you are involved in ministry, you will pray for and look for—until you find—someone with similar gifts and calling and disciple them into ministry, as you do ministry: on-the-job training. This is the Lord's calling and your assignment to pursue, intentionally, until you die. The result? Your church will grow exponentially as you do what Jesus did and as the New Testament apostles modeled. These changes occur in churches every time there is significant growth of the Christian faith. Church governance reform is often the beginning of that journey.

MAKEUP OF AN APOSTOLIC COUNSEL

Your church presently has some sort of decision-making group. These people should be led to realize that your congregation needs to move toward a more biblical form of church governance. They, along with everyone on staff, need to be committed to explore a better form of decision-making.

Leaders and staff will learn about the forms of church governance that exist. These were covered earlier in this book. Then, they should be involved in taking the Church Government Consultation Survey. This is the stage of "interrogative influence" discussed in Chapter Nine. Then, they should see the results. This is a gentle way of exploring a subject many church leaders have never considered.

While some members of the church are presently considered "leaders," as this process continues, (1) some may not be interested—or feel they are not qualified to serve in the new model of *apostolic counsel*; (2) the size of the *apostolic counsel* may require *fewer* leaders involved; and (3) there may be present leaders who have never discovered their spiritual gifts. Your staff and present leaders will decide which spiritual gift mix will be most beneficial for your church at this time in history.

The leader of the *apostolic counsel* is usually the (senior) pastor of the church. This leadership role is focused on: (1) biblical teaching; (2) discipling others; (3) agenda development; (4) recognizing when the group decision-making process is stalled on a particular issue; and (5) guiding counsel members toward a time of prayer and biblical reflection.

The size of the *apostolic counsel* differs from church to church. However, the range is usually four or five in smaller churches and as many as six to twelve in larger churches. This approach is focused on the spiritual *quality* of leadership, rather than quantity. Conceptually, the lens for constructing the *apostolic counsel* is not based on representation by age, gender, or numbers of those who serve. It is focused on those who have a history of commitment to Bible study, passion to search the Scripture for wisdom and guidance, and a cluster of spiritual gifts that will benefit the ministry of the counsel.

In the launch phase, if you have only four people, plus the pastor, to lead a congregation of a thousand in worship, it is fine. Again, the focus is on biblical and spiritual quality, not quantity. This concept may challenge some Christians. However, as you use this form of governance, you will see increased value for the work of God's Kingdom. Remember, in time, your *apostolic counsel* will be a discipling mechanism for more leaders.

The focus is on spiritual quality, not quantity.

WHAT ABOUT VOTING?

In politically oriented decision-making groups, voting seems like a "sacred" requirement. In the culture of an apostolic theocracy, decisions are always made by *unanimous consensus*. To repeat the Scripture, Acts 15:28 (NIV) says, "It seemed good to the Holy Spirit and to us...."

There may be those who immediately object: "We will never get anything accomplished." Yet, those leaders who have developed the culture of an apostolic theocracy have discovered that it is not only possible, but refreshing.

Who does this work? The leader of the *apostolic counsel* guides the group, monitoring the discussion on the subject. Sensing a *readiness for consensus*, the leaders say, "Does anyone object from a spiritual perspective?" If someone does object, it is a sign that consensus has not yet been achieved. The key dynamic is *respect* for each person and the group.

How does this work? Those who are not ready are given the opportunity to respectfully share their concerns. It is assumed that the discussion that follows will be based on a biblical perspective. If there are no concerns, the choices for next steps include prayer, searching Scripture, and respectful dialogue. If consensus is not reached, the issue is tabled with a plan to continue to pray, seek counsel from Scripture, and meet at a later date.

All matters should be decided by unanimous consensus. While some issues "require a vote" by governmental law, you can ask for a consensus vote. How does that work? The leader says, "By law, we must have a 'first' and a 'second' motion to make this decision." After that procedure is completed, the leader says, "From a spiritual perspective, does anyone object?" With no objection, the leader declares a "unanimous consensus," which is legally recorded. (If there is not unanimous consensus, it is understood that the *apostolic counsel* is not *ready* to make a decision. More prayer and Scripture study are required.)

While this approval sounds "impossible" to many when they first consider it, there are numerous *apostolic counsels* that have served effectively for years using this approach.

ADDING TO THE COUNSEL

One of the priorities for the pastor and counsel members is to be continually praying for and looking for—until you find—a potential person who is willing to be discipled for counsel leadership.

This approach—which is biblical—means the "disciple" would be "qualified": (1) have a gift mix that would benefit the counsel's work; (2) demonstrate a lifestyle priority for the study of Scripture; and (3) accept the discipling process in the Scripture, as modeled by Jesus. It includes six steps, discussed in Chapter Three: Step 1: Come follow me; Step 2: I do/you watch; Step 3: I do/you help; Step 4: You do/I help; Step 5: You do/I watch; Step 6: We both pray for and look for—until we find—another person to disciple.

Can you picture this? The pastor and five people make up the *apostolic counsel.* Further, each has one person they are discipling who sits next to them. Now there are five decision-makers who are, in the process, discipling five more. Will the counsel mushroom in size to an unwieldly number of people? No! The leaders are discipling other leaders, first and foremost. The disciples may become a replacement for their discipler. Or, they may become an addition to the counsel, bringing spiritual gifts that the original members did not have. They may become leaders in other ministries in the church. Imagine the spiritual value of multiplying apostolic leaders in other areas of your congregation's ministries: music, worship, Sunday school, women's and men's groups, Bible studies, youth, outreach efforts, hospital visitation, church planting, and in many more areas.

MAKING THE CHANGE

So, now it is time to make the change from a political form of church governance to an apostolic, Bible-based approach for decision-making. How do you do it?

First, you must use your present legal mechanism to make the decision to move forward. You will follow your present constitution. If that calls for a congregational vote, then you are required by law to do it. The decision is framed like this:

> "We have been in the process of reviewing the approach we use to make decisions. Our staff and leaders will be involved in a detailed survey that leads us to identify a biblical approach that would be more effective for our church.
>
> "Then, all our church members will have the opportunity to take the same survey. Here's what we will likely discover: In every church, a high percentage of the leadership group and the members choose the biblical approaches in every area of decision-making! Our staff and leadership believe we should try this scriptural form of decision-making, and we will propose an initial trial period."

Note: Some churches have chosen a six-month trial period. Others have elected to try it for as long as two years. Your staff and leaders will propose what seems right for your church. To make the decision, follow whatever approach your present constitution requires. As part of the decision, it is important to clarify the legality of this approach:

> "As we vote, everyone must be clear: We understand that our present constitution is the legal document we must honor. So, if we come to any serious legal impasse or issue, we must—for this 'trial period'—use our present constitution. However, we are collectively agreeing that for the normal decisions, we will try this *apostolic counsel* approach. Our approach is to put this new form of decision-making side by side with our legal document. However, during the trial period, for any legal issues, we will follow our constitution."

Then you will ask for approval, including whatever length of time you choose for the trial period. With this understanding, your church makes a "both/and" legal decision. Among the churches we have consulted through this process, 100 percent have agreed to try the *apostolic counsel* approach.

At the end of the trial period, this is the most frequent response from church leaders and members: "Why did we ever put up with the political approach of our old constitution? We feel liberated. This makes so much sense. We get so much more ministry accomplished—faster and easier."

Many churches are part of a larger denomination, fellowship, or network. Some of them require "approval" from someone in the larger church body for a replacement portion of the constitution. Once your church reshapes your constitution to fit the *apostolic counsel* approach, it is important to submit it for approval—if that is part of your larger denominational culture. At this level, 100 percent of the churches—from many types of larger church bodies—have received approval. Why? It is biblical!

You simply cannot improve on Scripture. This applies to many of the areas of ministry in your church. It will apply to your approach toward governance as well.

The more we have thoroughly studied ministry effectiveness, the more it becomes clear: The way we make decisions, the approach to governance, has a great impact on mission and ministry.

Your greatest decision: Would you like to experience the power and effectiveness of the New Testament Church you read about in Scripture? Your governance structure change is a huge step in that direction, as a church, denomination, mission agency, or parachurch ministry.

> "Don't worry about anything, but in all your prayers ask God for what you need, always asking him with a thankful heart. And God's peace, which is far beyond human understanding, will keep your hearts and minds safe in union with Christ Jesus."
>
> —Philippians 4:6-7 [2]

Reflective Questions for Chapter Ten: Launching a Biblical Approach

1. Most people find change difficult. Christians are not exempt from that challenge. When you want and need to make important changes, it often helps to have an "interventionist." For example, it required some great advice from my doctor for me to lose some weight. Do you think, with help from the outside, your church could travel the path to more effective decision-making? If so, how would you go about it?

2. Almost every church has at least one "church bully." Those types of people are often overconfident, opinionated, and forceful in their approach. They may be absent in Bible study, yet visible at church meetings. How do you react? Do you pray for them? Do you try to get to know them? Do you try to help them grow spiritually? Do you point to Jesus—the One who met Saul (later called Paul) on the Damascus road?

3. When you serve in your church, do you see it as a part of your Christian *calling*? Does that service bring you joy and fulfillment? Or, do you feel obligated because someone has asked you or the church "needs the job done"? Do you know your unique spiritual gifts, given by the Holy Spirit? Have you discovered where God wants you to serve? If you haven't, your service becomes a job, not a joy. If you have discovered your gifts, your service is a joy, not a job! Where are you?

4. The way your church makes decisions has great impact on the effectiveness of the ministry. Is your church growing? Is it reaching people who are far from God? Are new Christians being discipled? Are leaders making spiritual decisions based on Scripture and prayer? Is the decision-making process uplifting and joyful, uniting the body of Christ and glorifying Jesus? How you answer these questions will reveal your commitment to a biblical form of church governance.

ACKNOWLEDGMENTS

Alongside every author is a team of those who support, encourage, and add to the long process of writing a book. The task includes multiple edits, input, encouragement, and critique, as well as formatting, smooth writing, and all the rest.

I'm grateful for our leader at Church Doctor Ministries, Tracee J. Swank, whose name appears on the front cover and without whom this book and our work with churches would never occur.

I thank God for my patient and persevering wife, Janet, who spent numerous hours in the final edit copies of the manuscript.

I thank God for Jason Atkinson, my valuable assistant and partner in ministry projects.

I'm also grateful to God for the Church Doctor Ministries team who has served during the development of this work: Katie Erickson, Chelsey Genszler, Matt Genszler, Jason Atkinson, Carol Hart, Beth Knoll, Becca Shrom, and John Wargowsky.

I greatly appreciate the impact from three special friends—Paul Griebel, Frank Grepke, and Bob Shriner—who read the manuscript in an earlier form and provided important feedback and encouragement.

I thank God for many others who have published various works on the general subject of church governance and who have challenged me to go deeper on this important topic.

It has been my privilege to consult numerous churches and guide them through governance transformation and a biblical approach to decision-making. It is so gratifying to see God's people liberated from politics that no longer frustrate and divides ministry.

ENDNOTES

Introduction

1. Warren, Rick. Introduction to *An Unstoppable Force: Daring to Become the Church God Had in Mind* by Erwin McManus. Loveland, CO: Flagship Church Resources (Group Publishing Inc.), 2001, pp. 6-7.

2. Hoag, Gary G., Wesley K. Willmer, and Gregory J. Henson. *The Council: A Biblical Perspective on Board Governance*. Winchester, VA: ECFAPress, 2018, page 21.

3. Hunter, Kent R. *Your Church Has Personality: Find Your Focus—Maximize Your Mission*. Corunna, IN: Church Growth Center, 1997.

4. John 18:36.

Chapter One: Church Alive!

1. John 18:36. *New International Version Bible*, Colorado Springs, CO: Biblica, Inc., 2011.

2. Hunter, Kent R., with Tracee J. Swank. *Who Broke My Church? 7 Proven Strategies for Renewal and Revival*. New York: Hachette Book Group/FaithWords, 2017, pp. 62-64.

Chapter Two: But We've Always Done It That Way!

1. Since the church is part of the "body of Christ," there is, or should be, continuity in mission direction. Churches have a common mission, given by Jesus, to "make disciples of all nations" (technically, "all peoples" or "people groups").

   In addition, every church, like every person, has its own unique "personality." While the mission among churches is consistent, the personality of each local church is determined by the type of people in the church, its location, and those in the immediate community—your primary mission field.

   In my book *Your Church Has Personality: Find Your Focus—Maximize Your Mission*, I urge every congregation to develop their own unique philosophy of ministry statement. This short document describes the uniqueness of your church. It is a tool that helps those you reach know the unique personality of your church. It is a tool that helps new people to know if your church is a good "fit" for them. A philosophy of ministry statement will help you grow your church.

Chapter Three: Apostolic Theocracy: Organizational Control or Movement?

1. Robert III, Henry M., Daniel H. Honemann, Thomas J. Balch, Daniel E. Seabold, and Shmuel Gerber. *Robert's Rules of Order Newly Revised 12th Edition*. New York: PublicAffairs, 2020.

2. This will be described in more detail in Chapter Seven.

3. John 3:8.

4. Lin, Johnny. "On the Use of Robert's Rules of Order in Churches - Johnny Lin," May 25, 2010. https://www.johnny-lin.com/papers/rules.pdf.

5. 1 Peter 4:1-2. *The Message: The Bible in Contemporary Language.* Colorado Springs, CO: NavPress, 2002.

6. Proverbs 15:22. *Revised Standard Version of the Bible.* Division of Christian Education of the National Council of the Churches of Christ in the United States of America, 1971.

7. We will focus on the scriptural difference between "councils" and "counsels" in Chapter Five.

8. Galatians 5:22-23. *New International Version Bible*, Colorado Springs, CO: Biblica, Inc., 2011.

9. Numbers 11:16-17.

10. Acts 15:28. *New International Version Bible*, Colorado Springs, CO: Biblica, Inc., 2011.

Chapter Four: Developing a Leadership Team

1. John 18:36. *The Message: The Bible in Contemporary Language.* Colorado Springs, CO: NavPress, 2002.

2. I have written about how to develop a philosophy of ministry for your church in the book *Your Church Has Personality: Find Your Focus—Maximize Your Mission.* Corunna, IN: Church Growth Center, 1997.

3. Acts 26:10. *The Holy Bible, Good News Translation.* New York: American Bible Society, 1992.

4. See my book *Your Spiritual Gifts: Discover God's Plan for Your Life.* Corunna, IN: Church Doctor Ministries, 2018.

Chapter Five: Council or Counsel?

1. Matthew 10:17. *New King James Version Bible*, Nashville, TN: Thomas Nelson Publishers, 1982.
2. Matthew 6:33. *New International Version Bible*, Colorado Springs, CO: Biblica, Inc., 2011.
3. Matthew 6:10. *New International Version Bible*, Colorado Springs, CO: Biblica, Inc., 2011.
4. John 18:36. *Revised Standard Version of the Bible*. Division of Christian Education of the National Council of the Churches of Christ in the United States of America, 1971.
5. Matthew 6:10. *New International Version Bible*, Colorado Springs, CO: Biblica, Inc., 2011.
6. Matthew 10:17. *New King James Version Bible*, Nashville, TN: Thomas Nelson Publishers, 1982.
7. Matthew 26:59. *The Holy Bible, English Standard Version*. Wheaton, IL: Good News Publishers, 2001.
8. Acts 5:27-28. *The Holy Bible, English Standard Version*. Wheaton, IL: Good News Publishers, 2001 (parenthesis mine).
9. Acts 5:34a, 38-39. *The Holy Bible, English Standard Version*. Wheaton, IL: Good News Publishers, 2001.
10. Acts 20:27. *The Holy Bible, English Standard Version*. Wheaton, IL: Good News Publishers, 2001 (emphasis mine).
11. Ephesians 1:11-12. *Revised Standard Version of the Bible*. Division of Christian Education of the National Council of the Churches of Christ in the United States of America, 1971 (emphasis mine).
12. Acts 8:20. *New International Version Bible*, Colorado Springs, CO: Biblica, Inc., 2011.

13. See Luke 7:30; Acts 2:23; Acts 4:28; Acts 5:38; Acts 20:27; Ephesians 1:11.

14. Isaiah 9:6. *The Holy Bible, English Standard Version*. Wheaton, IL: Good News Publishers, 2001 (emphasis mine).

15. John 14:15-17. *The Christian Standard Bible*. Nashville, TN: Holman Bible Publishers, 2017 (emphasis mine).

Chapter Six: Appointing *Apostolic Counsel* Members

1. Matthew 6:10 (my paraphrase).

2. Matthew 6:33. *New International Version Bible*, Colorado Springs, CO: Biblica, Inc., 2011.

3. John 20:21 (my paraphrase).

4. 1 Corinthians 1:10. *Revised Standard Version of the Bible*. Division of Christian Education of the National Council of the Churches of Christ in the United States of America, 1971.

5. John 3:30. *New International Version Bible*, Colorado Springs, CO: Biblica, Inc., 2011.

6. A thorough treatment of spiritual gifts can be found in my book *Your Spiritual Gifts: Discover God's Plan for Your Life*, Corunna, IN: Church Doctor Publishing, 2018.

Chapter Seven: Jesus' Dynamic Approach

1. Hunter, Kent R. *Your Spiritual Gifts: Discover God's Plan for Your Life*. Corunna, IN: Church Doctor Publishing, 2018. (This book includes two spiritual gift surveys, one for you to take on yourself and one for another Christian to take *about* you to get

another perspective.) Church Doctor Ministries also offers workshops that teach about spiritual gifts.

2. Some churches use a Church Doctor consultant or some other outside leader to guide those in the process of identifying the gift mix that will most effectively serve your congregation (www.churchdoctor.org).

3. This discipleship process is explained in depth in our book *Who Broke My Church? 7 Proven Strategies for Renewal and Revival*. New York: Hachette/FaithWords, 2017, pp. 162-170.

Chapter Eight: Transforming Your Church to an Apostolic Theocracy

1. Matthew 6:10b. *New International Version Bible*, Colorado Springs, CO: Biblica, Inc., 2011.

2. Isaiah 9:6. *The Holy Bible, English Standard Version*. Wheaton, IL: Good News Publishers, 2001.

3. Matthew 16:18. *Revised Standard Version of the Bible*. Division of Christian Education of the National Council of the Churches of Christ in the United States of America, 1971.

4. Romans 12:2. *Revised Standard Version of the Bible*. Division of Christian Education of the National Council of the Churches of Christ in the United States of America, 1971.

5. John 1:12. *Revised Standard Version of the Bible*. Division of Christian Education of the National Council of the Churches of Christ in the United States of America, 1971.

6. See 1 Peter 2:9. *Revised Standard Version of the Bible*. Division of Christian Education of the National Council of the Churches of Christ in the United States of America, 1971.

7. See Matthew 4:19. *Revised Standard Version of the Bible*. Division of Christian Education of the National Council of the Churches of Christ in the United States of America, 1971.

8. Wagner, C. Peter. *Leading Your Church to Growth: The Secret of Pastor/People Partnership in Dynamic Church Growth*. Ventura, CA: Regal Books: A Division of GL Publications, 1984, pp. 131-137.

Chapter Nine: Functions of Decision-Making

1. Matthew 16:15. *New International Version Bible*, Colorado Springs, CO: Biblica, Inc., 2011.

2. John 18:36. *New International Version Bible*, Colorado Springs, CO: Biblica, Inc., 2011, (parenthesis mine).

3. Ephesians 4:12. *Revised Standard Version of the Bible*. Division of Christian Education of the National Council of the Churches of Christ in the United States of America, 1971.

4. Once an apostolic theocracy style frees a church to reach its mission potential, the next step is to train those members who are ready (called "early adopters") to become missionaries to those in their social networks who are not yet Christ-followers. When the church is ready, we introduce them to the SEND movement (www.thesendmovement.com).

Chapter Ten: Launching a Biblical Approach

1. For over thirty-five years, the Church Doctor Ministries board of directors has served as a nonprofit and operated as an apostolic theocracy. Board members from many different states and from various Christian backgrounds have unanimously reported the approach as refreshing.

We have also worked with other nonprofit Christian ministries and led them through the process toward an apostolic theocracy.

The churches we have served to change to the apostolic theocracy model are from a wide variety of denominational, nondenominational, and unique theological backgrounds. They have flourished with this biblical approach as well.

2. Philippians 4:6-7. *Good News Translation of the Bible*. New York: American Bible Society, 1992.

Focused Message + Disciplined Strategy = Mission Momentum

Your formula for clear communication, expanded influence, and increased joy in ministry

Cast a Clear & Compelling Vision

Clarify your mission and message and watch your church grow in health and vitality.

Increase Engagement

Clear communication in ministry allows more people to connect with who you are and what you do.

Reduce Friction & Frustration

Find joy in ministry again and stop spinning your wheels with outdated methods.

We know how difficult it is for a church to reach people in a noisy, distracted world. That is why we focus only on serving churches and nonprofit ministries. We know you. We have your back.

1. **Schedule a Call**
2. **Create a Customized Plan**
3. **Implement Systems From Your Plan**
4. **Receive Ongoing Coaching and Follow-Up**

CHURCH DOCTOR MINISTRIES

ClarifyYourMinistryMessage.com
Talk to a guide: (800) 626-8515

Made in the USA
Monee, IL
13 October 2024

67156416R00085